Bio-Nutrionics

Bio-Nutrionics

Lower Your Cholesterol in 30 Days

by Emanuel Cheraskin, M.D., D.M.D.,
and Neil S. Orenstein, Ph.D.,
with Paul L. Miner

A Perigee Book

Perigee Books
are published by
The Putnam Publishing Group
200 Madison Avenue
New York, NY 10016

Library of Congress Cataloging-in-Publication Data

Cheraskin, E. (Emanuel), date.
Bio-nutrionics: lower your cholesterol in 30 days.

"A Perigee original."
Bibliography: p.
1. Low-cholesterol diet. 2. Exercise therapy.
3. Low-choloesterol diet—Recipes. I. Orenstein,
Neil S. II. Miner, Paul L. [DNLM: 1. Cholesterol,
Dietary—popular works. 2. Cookery. WB 425 C521b]
RM237.75.C48   1986   613.2'8   86-9399
ISBN 0-399-51268-3

Printed in the United States of America
1 2 3 4 5 6 7 8 9 10

Acknowledgments

Antonia Villi Miner for her contribution in originating, adapting and organizing the recipe section of this book.

Diane Borho, Maureen Byrne, Sandy Hirsch, Paula Shabman, and Sondra Tarica—all nutritionists at Bio-Nutrionics, New York City.

Dr. William Castelli for his gracious response to interviews and information in preparation of the manuscript.

Stanley J. Leifer, president of Bio-Nutrionics, Inc., who skillfully pulled together all the individuals responsible for this book.

Giant Foods Corporation
The American Heart Association
The U.S. Department of Agriculture
The National Heart, Lung and Blood Institute
Dr. Donald Rudin and Mrs. Rudin
Ayers Art Studio of Baltimore, graphics

And to our editor, Judy Linden, for her skill, patience and enthusiasm for this project.

A special thanks for selected recipes from The Culinary Arts Center, Lenox, MA, Sarah L. Bingham, M.S., Director.

To Dr. Jeffrey S. Bland who taught me much about nutritional biochemistry, and to Sarah L. Bingham who taught me much about the nutritional value of foods.

—NSO

To my wife, Antonia, for her support and encouragement.

—PLM

Contents

Introduction   **15**

The Promise of This Book · Bio-Nutrionics—The Physician's Plan · The Benefits of the New York City Program Come to You · How the Bio-Nutrionics Concept Started · Take This Book Seriously · It Takes a Very Short Time to See Positive Results

1. Cholesterol Overload: The Enemy of Your Health   **23**

What Is Cholesterol Overload? · What Is CHD? · What Is Cholesterol? · How Cholesterol Is "Packaged" in the Body · How Cholesterol Causes Atherosclerosis · Coronary Atherosclerosis and Heart Attacks · Most People's Cholesterol Is Excessively High

2. Cholesterol and CHD: The Cause-and-Effect Relationship   **33**

Unraveling the Mystery of CHD · When Are You at Serious Risk? · Other Risk Indicators · The Proof That CHD Can Be Prevented · Are You a Candidate for CHD? · Everyone Should Think About Reducing His or Her Risk · Bio-Nutrionics: The Good News

3. The Bio-Nutrionics Program to Cholesterol Reduction   **45**

Your Personal Risk Analysis Questionnaire · Getting Motivated · How the Program Works · Smoking

4. The Nutrition Plan   **55**

Foods to Eat and Foods to Avoid · The Fats in Our Diet · Avoid Foods That Are Processed and Contain Refined Sugar · Fiber in Our Diet · Plan Your Daily Meals

from Six Food Groups · Calories Count—But You Don't
Have to Count Them · How to Find Your Recommended
Weight and Plan Your Daily Menus · Understanding Vi-
tamins and Minerals · There's Nothing Better Than a
Healthy Diet

5. Putting the Nutrition Plan to Work   **91**
Tip Sheet · Menu Planning · Stocking Up · Recipe
Index · How to Assert Yourself in a Restaurant

6. Physical Activity   **153**
Add Physical Activity to Nutrition for Fast Results · Get
Up and Get Active · The Remarkable Benefits of Walk-
ing · Exercise Regularly · Chart Your Progress

7. The Bottom Line   **161**
You Can Prevent Cholesterol Overload · The Proof of the
Promise · More Proof of the Promise · It's Your Turn to
Prove the Promise

Glossary   169
A Personal Nutritionist for a Fraction of Normal
   Cost   171
Bibliography   173

Bio-Nutrionics

Introduction

THE PROMISE OF THIS BOOK

By following the program outlined here you *can* lower your high blood cholesterol in thirty days without the aid of medication of any kind. You also will begin to reach your ideal weight for your height and build; regain energy, stamina, and vitality you may not have felt in years; and—most important—dramatically reduce your risk factors for cardiovascular disease. We guarantee you will feel terrific! With these improvements, you can't help but have a more positive attitude . . . be more confident and self-assured.

Bio-Nutrionics is *not* a diet book. "Diet" implies deprivation, and you will not be deprived of foods that are delicious and good for you. It is a unique easy-to-follow program, based on a physician's plan given at the Bio-Nutrionics Center in New York City, that embraces nutrition, physical activity, and mental outlook—a "wellness" program containing all the variables that contribute to good health.

Already endorsed by thousands of people, including world champion tennis player Ivan Lendl, Bio-Nutrionics is a proven plan that produces results in a short but realistic period of time. These results are so significant that they prompted us to write this book. We want you, too, to discover the difference Bio-Nutrionics can make.

The role nutrition plays in our basic good health has been overlooked for the past several decades. We've been brought up to believe that plenty of red meat is good for us. We were taught that a healthy breakfast is a plate of bacon and eggs. We've overconsumed dairy products and replaced basic grains in our daily bread with a soft, puffy white substance that has been stripped of most all its nutrients. Remember the scenes of our Western cowboys driving cattle to market? They didn't eat the critters! The protein these lean and energetic men survived on was beans!

This book is written clearly and is easy to understand. It is not meant to be a scientific exposition, but rather a lifetime plan to help improve your health.

We are, however, dealing with a subject that sometimes requires technical words and phrases. The human body is a complex biochemical machine and scientists have created a language of their own to describe the actions of food, physical activity, and medication on the body. Some words describing these responses play an important role in explaining the Bio-Nutrionics Program, and we have tried to define them in the text. As a further guide a glossary is included beginning on page 169.

While we have great respect for documented scientific proof, we also value common sense. For example, although we address high cholesterol, common sense tells us that anything in extreme is harmful. For this reason, we don't want to ignore that some people may have low cholesterol. We'll show how Bio-Nutrionics helps these individuals very briefly in Chapter 7.

We also recognize that no one will stick to a program that is too strict. So we accommodate individual likes, dislikes, and indulgences from time to time. A heaping plate of pasta, a dish of frozen yogurt, a glass of wine or beer with dinner are all part of our eating plan.

BIO-NUTRIONICS—THE PHYSICIAN'S PLAN

A person entering the Bio-Nutrionics program in New York City fills out an extensive questionnaire about their health, personal dietary habits, physical activity, and lifestyle. Each participant receives a blood test and urinalysis. Their blood pressure, resting pulse, pulse after exercise, and the amount of time it takes to return to resting pulse are all recorded by a technician working under the direction of a physician. A consultation with a professional nutritionist is also a part of this first meeting.

All the data gathered from a client's tests and his questionnaire is fed into the Bio-Nutrionics computer. Within ten days a printout is prepared. The printout contains a customized and personalized report and recommendations. Each individual gets a complete analysis of his physical examination, urinalysis, and blood tests including cholesterol levels and ratios. There is a health-risk index report that suggests how specific diet and lifestyle changes can reduce risk factors for illness and disease. There also is a complete nutritional evaluation. This becomes the basis for planning a new eating program that allows you to select an assortment of delicious items from six food groups. Your current level of daily physical activity is evaluated and you receive recommendations for a regular yet unrestricted activity program that fits into your life-style. Clients have frequent consultations with the nutritionist assigned to them who carefully monitors their progress. Between personal meetings (and there may be as many as seven in the first month of the program), clients can call by phone for consultation and advice.

Thirty days after the program begins, clients repeat the identical series of tests, so that their progress can be measured. After that, they continue the program independently.

THE BENEFITS OF THE NEW YORK CITY PROGRAM COME TO YOU

Lowering your cholesterol in thirty days is just one beneficial consequence of the New York program which we've chosen to detail in this book. It's similar to the master Bio-Nutrionics Program in a number of ways. First, the end result will be overall good health. Second, the book contains a questionnaire for you to fill out. It will help you judge your risk factors for coronary heart disease. Third, your analysis will guide you in the way to use the recommended food lists, adapted from the main program. At the end of thirty days, you are asked to complete an identical questionnaire that will measure your progress. You then can judge for yourself the benefits gained.

HOW THE BIO-NUTRIONICS CONCEPT STARTED

In 1980, Franc M. Ricciardi, chairman and president of Richton International Corporation, was stricken with classic angina symptoms. His chest pains were severe and he was admitted as an emergency patient in a coronary intensive-care unit. To aid their diagnosis, doctors scheduled an angiogram. During this invasive diagnostic procedure, Ricciardi had a heart attack and had to undergo an emergency coronary bypass operation. The operation was complicated by an open-flap heart valve; Ricciardi was not expected to survive. Fortunately for all of us he did.

But Franc's recovery was slow and he found the drugs the doctors prescribed for his heart condition enervating. He became seriously disturbed over his lack of stamina and energy. A friend suggested he see a nutritionist. "There's no reason for you to be so tired all the time. A change in your food habits may help you in the same way it did me." The friend recommended a well-known program. Although Ricciardi barely knew what a nutritionist was, he was willing to try anything to recover his stamina.

The first program he tried helped him feel better, but he found its food and life-style requirement too spartan. The change in diet, however, brought about enough of a change in the way he felt to convince him that there was a better way to regain his health than by relying on doctor-prescribed drugs alone. Ricciardi set out to find that better way. He tried several other programs, but none quite measured up to his expectations. Finally, he heard about Dr. Robert Haas, whose personalized nutrition programs seemed to be performing near miracles for tennis star Martina Navratilova and others. Haas developed a personalized nutrition program for Ricciardi that improved his health, increased his stamina, and changed his entire outlook on life.

Ricciardi wanted to share his good fortune with anyone concerned about his or her health, but realized that seeing a nutritionist like Haas on a one-to-one basis could be too expensive for the average person. He looked to modern computer technology for the answer. He organized a team of physicians, biochemists, registered dieticians, and nutritionists to further develop and add the latest nutritional information to the original Haas plan. A computer program was created that could aid doctors in the analysis of an individual's health and nutrition problems and the planning of his or her health, life-style, and nutrition program—a *personalized* approach at an affordable cost.

And so Bio-Nutrionics was born. Founded on the principle that everyone is biochemically unique—that is, that each of us is different than every other person in the world—it is today helping thousands of people improve their quality of life.

As mentioned previously one of those people is twenty-five-year-old world-class tennis champion Ivan Lendl. Previously defeated on the courts more often by fatigue than by his opponents, Lendl needed help. A life-style analysis by Dr. Robert Haas showed his diet to be so exceptionally high in fats that he was sleeping between ten and twelve hours per day! Breakfast consisted of four to six eggs with bacon or sausage, while lunch and dinner were usually fast-food cheeseburgers or fried chicken nuggets washed down with soft drinks. Lendl never touched vegetables and did not eat fruit on a regular basis. No wonder his serum cholesterol level was in the high-risk range at a shocking 275!

After a year of living—and eating—the Bio-Nutrionics way, Lendl claims he is playing better tennis and winning more tournaments than ever before. In fact, in September 1985, Lendl conquered John McEnroe at the prestigious U.S. Open, an event where he failed previously to make the finals for three years in a row. In January 1986 his number-one ranking was assured after winning the Nabisco Masters, his thirty-fifth victory of his last thirty-six matches.

Not only had the Bio-Nutrionics way of life increased Lendl's endurance, but his cholesterol level dropped to 150, he lost fifteen pounds, and he needs only eight hours of sleep a night when he is playing tennis and three to four hours when he's not. You will see results, too, if you make a conscientious commitment to our program.

TAKE THIS BOOK SERIOUSLY

If you do, it will fulfill its promise.

Our most recent study of 104 male and 64 female subjects on the Bio-Nutrionics Program with an age range between fifteen and seventy-five (a mean age of forty-two) shows an average reduction of cholesterol of 10 percent in the first thirty days of the program.

What does this mean to you? According to medical authorities, a 1 percent reduction in blood cholesterol results in a *2 percent reduction* in *coronary risk*. Therefore, the people on the plan reduced their risk of cardiovascular diseases (which include high blood pressure, stroke, and coronary disease) by 20 percent in thirty days!

We ask that you make a serious commitment to your own personal health and well-being. The life-style modifications outlined in this book are not drastic and they *will* work for you. But they do require your complete participation to be effective. The most important qualification you need to succeed is the determination to take control of your own health. And you're worth it!

IT TAKES A VERY SHORT TIME TO SEE
POSITIVE RESULTS

Your cholesterol reduction may start more quickly than you expect. Certain food elements in the nutrition program are known to work almost immediately to reduce high cholesterol. For example, the Bio-Nutrionics Program recommends you eat oat bran cereal and oat bran muffins because research has demonstrated that in some individuals these foods can reduce cholesterol by as much as 10 percent in a single month. The reduction occurs even though no other nutritional changes are made. You will be eating a diet rich in vitamin C. There is ample scientific evidence that vitamin C will reduce cholesterol quickly. You will sharply reduce your intake of saturated fats, a dietary change that results in cholesterol reduction. The Bio-Nutrionics Program incorporates all of these individual cholesterol reducers into a balanced daily eating plan. Not only will you lower your high cholesterol but you will discover a "preventive maintenance" life plan that will keep you fit no matter what your age.

Before starting the program you should know what cholesterol is and understand its role in coronary heart disease.

1. Cholesterol Overload: The Enemy of Your Health

WHAT IS CHOLESTEROL OVERLOAD?

There is overwhelming evidence that Americans and people who live in the more affluent nations of the world are suffering and dying from the overconsumption of high-fat, nutrient-deficient foods. This leads to what we call "Cholesterol Overload."

The medical term for this affliction is "hypercholesterolemia." It means we have more cholesterol in our blood than is consistent with good health. This may be the result of eating too many high-cholesterol foods or the body producing too much or eliminating too little cholesterol.

Cholesterol overload is the first stage of a condition that progressively leads to atherosclerosis, commonly called hardening of the arteries. Atherosclerosis in turn contributes to coronary heart disease, or CHD.

WHAT IS CHD?

CHD is also called coronary artery disease and cardiovascular disease. All three names describe a coronary

artery disease that results from the buildup of plaque—
a substance that contains cholesterol—on the inside walls
of arteries leading to the heart. Coronary atherosclerosis
occurs when the buildup gradually fills the inner chan-
nel of arteries and causes them to become firm, inflex-
ible, and narrower. The symptoms of CHD may appear
as the flow of nutrients and blood to the heart is slowed
or cut off. One symptom is angina, a severe or mild pain
that may be felt as a heavy or tight sensation in the breast,
or as a pain in the left arm or the left side of the chest
or neck. The pains may be accompanied by a general
feeling of discomfort and shortness of breath. CHD is
a degenerative disease that in its later stages can lead to
a heart attack or stroke. In fact, CHD is the cause of
one out of every three deaths in the United States, and
kills one American *every* minute. Forty-three and a half
million of us have CHD to one degree or another at this
very moment. This year alone a million and a half people
will suffer heart attacks.

We, as well as medical authorities around the world,
believe that many of these victims can be saved by a
program that reduces and controls their cholesterol
overload. It's easy and we'll soon show you how.

WHAT IS CHOLESTEROL?

Cholesterol is a white, sticky, fatlike, tasteless and odor-
less substance necessary to all of our cells. It is carried
in our bloodstream, and found in all foods of animal
origin.

From the day we're born we begin taking cholesterol
into our body in the foods we eat. That is one source of
cholesterol.

Our second source of cholesterol is the body itself,
which produces a steady supply of it in our intestinal

tract and in our liver. Day in and day out throughout our lifetime we continue this process of both ingesting and manufacturing cholesterol. When we eat high quantities of cholesterol the body responds by manufacturing less. When we eat too little cholesterol the body responds by producing more. Remarkable, isn't it?

Cholesterol Is Important to Overall Health

Cholesterol serves as raw material for the creation of cell membranes, bile acids, and sex hormones. Nine tenths of all the cholesterol in our bodies is located in the cells. A major part of our total cholesterol supply is used in the continuous process of regenerating and rebuilding body cells.

Some of us think of "serum cholesterol" when we hear the word "cholesterol." Another commonly used term is "blood cholesterol." For our purposes, the meaning is the same.

Your doctor may have reported to you that your cholesterol level (or reading) is "normal," "moderate," or "high." He is speaking of serum cholesterol. Serum cholesterol can be measured. It is generally held that the most accurate measurements are taken after fasting for twelve hours. Cholesterol tests usually are performed as part of a standard profile of blood tests which are incorporated into most annual physical checkups and other routine office examinations.

How Cholesterol Readings Are Taken

Blood is drawn and allowed to clot. The clotted solids are removed. The liquid that remains is the serum that contains cholesterol. The amount of cholesterol is measured in milligrams per deciliter of blood. (A deciliter is one hundred milliliters or one-tenth of a liter. It is equal to about 3.4 fluid ounces.) A cholesterol level of 200 means that your blood sample contains 200 milligrams of cholesterol per deciliter of blood. The cholesterol number is written as 200 mg/dl. (Throughout this book we will drop mg/dl and use the cholesterol number by itself.)

This method of measurement allows medical researchers to compare your cholesterol level at one period of time with a level measured at an earlier or later date. It is also possible to compare various groups of people living in different areas with different diets, habits, and life-styles. This type of study is called an epidemiological study.

HOW CHOLESTEROL IS "PACKAGED" IN THE BODY

Cholesterol is packaged by the body so it can be transported through the arteries, into the capillaries, and finally into the cells. These packages are called lipoproteins—a medical term that means a combination of fats and proteins. Three of these lipoprotein packages play a prominent role in the way cholesterol functions in the body.

Three Lipoprotein Packages

The first of the three lipoproteins is HDL, or high-density lipoprotein. It may sound like a complicated scientific name at first but it really is quite simple. "High-density" means that the lipid, or fat, particles, and the protein particles it is composed of, are dense and heavy. They tend to cling or stick together. These high-density lipoproteins travel through the bloodstream to the capillaries and into the body tissue to build cell membranes, bile acids, and sex hormones. HDL cholesterol is beneficial and considered protective to the arteries and heart. It is commonly called the "good" cholesterol. The more HDL you have in your body, the lower your risk of developing CHD.

The second package of lipoprotein is LDL, for low-density lipoprotein. LDLs are thought to be a major cause of cholesterol deposits in coronary arteries. In LDLs the fat portion does not cling or stick to the "package" while being transported through the bloodstream. When the LDLs separate, the fat sticky substances attach themselves to the interior walls of arteries. LDLs also cause the body's cholesterol production to become abnormally high.

The third lipoprotein is VLDL, for very low-density lipoproteins. Researchers know less about VLDL cholesterol than they do about either HDL or LDL. VLDLs play a lesser role than LDLs in the risk of developing cholesterol deposits in blood vessels.

Although when seen from the outside, an artery may appear to be quite large, there are places where the inside diameter of a human coronary artery is only two millimeters ($^1/_{12}$ inch). A cholesterol buildup—a blockage no larger than a BB shot—can close off the blood flow and so cut off the heart's supply of oxygen and nourishment and cause a heart attack.

The diagrams below show how cholesterol buildup causes blockages that cut off the blood supply to the heart.

The diagram on the left shows a cross-section view of a clear artery. The diagram on the right is a view of the identical artery after the buildup of cholesterol-containing plaque.

The diagram on the left shows a side view of a clear artery. The diagram on the right is a view of the identical artery after the buildup of plaque and cholesterol.

HOW CHOLESTEROL CAUSES ATHEROSCLEROSIS

Atherosclerosis is a degenerative disease that restricts arteries throughout the body, but can be especially dangerous when it affects those leading to the heart and the brain. As mentioned previously, the common name for this process is hardening of the arteries. Atherosclerosis usually starts early in life and by middle age most individuals have it to one degree or another.

The low-density lipoproteins, the LDL cholesterol, helps start the artery-hardening process. Many researchers believe that LDL cholesterol is attracted, as if by a magnet, to torn, scarred, or damaged areas of the interior walls of arteries, known as lesions. They are caused by tiny pieces of hardened plaque, crystallized cholesterol, or other hardened chemical substances circulating in the bloodstream. The tiny deposits of LDL attached to the lesions seem to work like the single grain of sand that eventually becomes the pearl in the oyster. The first tiny deposit of cholesterol attracts plaque, debris, calcium deposits, and additional fat as they pass by in the bloodstream. Gradually damlike blockages form, grow larger, and harden. Coronary arteries lose their ability to expand and contract. And the blood begins to move sluggishly through the narrowed arteries. Slowly the interior channels of blocked and hardened arteries continue to narrow and as a result the blood suppy to the heart is reduced.

Cholesterol buildup can progress over years before any overt symptoms appear.

CORONARY ATHEROSCLEROSIS AND HEART ATTACKS

A coronary artery that becomes completely blocked cuts off the blood supply to the heart. Without oxygen and nourishment from the blood, the heart muscle quickly dies. This is a heart attack.

Atherosclerosis and High Blood Pressure

As atherosclerosis advances arteries become increasingly narrow. When the heart is forced to work harder and harder to pump blood through the narrowed openings, blood pressure rises. High blood pressure is a warning, a signal, a symptom that may foretell a stroke. A stroke occurs when there is a loss of blood supply to the brain. Like the heart muscle, brain cells require a continuous supply of nourishment and oxygen from the blood. When the blood supply is cut off by a blockage, brain cells begin to die. The immediate result is brain injury; within six minutes death occurs. People with a history of heart disease and people with high blood pressure are especially vulnerable to strokes. So are people who are overweight, who are inactive, and people with diabetes.

Over 500,000 Americans are stroke victims each year. The death rate from stroke is almost 170,000 annually.

MOST PEOPLE'S CHOLESTEROL IS
EXCESSIVELY HIGH

Research reveals that far more people than ever suspected are at high risk of heart attack and stroke because of cholesterol overload. For years many of us have been assured by our doctors that our cholesterol levels were "within normal range." With that assurance we paid little attention to our blood cholesterol level until it reached 250 or higher. At that point our doctor usually sounded the alarm and we searched frantically to find a way to undo the damage. But by 1984, it was accepted that excessive buildup of fats and cholesterol in our arteries is a primary cause of coronary artery disease. The time had finally arrived for the medical establishment to mount an all-out campaign against the nation's number-one killer.

In December 1984 the National Heart, Lung and Blood Institute and the Office of Medical Applications of Research convened a Consensus Development Conference on Lowering Blood Cholesterol to Prevent Heart Disease. The report, developed after analyzing extensive worldwide research data, stated that millions of people who previously had believed they were at only moderate risk of heart disease suddenly found themselves in a much higher risk category.

The chart on page 31 shows existing cholesterol levels in adult males and the recommended, or safe, cholesterol levels for the same group.

The broken line on the right shows that the mean cholesterol level for an adult American male is currently at 210. A "safe" cholesterol level is in the 150–170 range. Dr. William Castelli, director of the Framingham Study (see page 34), has stated that he has never seen a case of CHD in an individual whose cholesterol level is at 150 or lower.

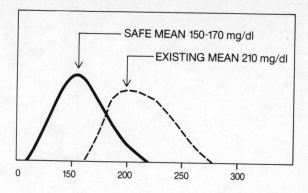

Women and CHD

Most charts and studies of CHD deal with men because they are statistically more likely to be victims of the disease. So it's natural to assume women are protected somehow from premature heart disease. The fact is, CHD is the number-one cause of death in women as well as men. Don't forget that everything in this program applies to men and women equally.

2. Cholesterol and CHD: The Cause-and-Effect Relationship

UNRAVELING THE MYSTERY OF CHD

It has taken thirty-five years of research and untold millions of dollars to finally establish a definite cause-and-effect relationship between cholesterol and CHD. Unraveling the mystery of the causes of coronary heart disease has been one of the great challenges of medicine. In the process there have been studies of entire populations; studies within populations; animal studies; and human intervention studies. While some of this research has led to clear-cut conclusions, other results have often left researchers baffled.

One reason for the difficulty in establishing a cause-and-effect relationship between the disease and a single specific factor is because CHD is what we call a multifactorial disease. A great many factors, including dietary deficiencies and excesses, personality characteristics, lifestyle patterns, and heredity play a part in either causing or advancing the disease.

In 1981 doctors at the Cardiology Division of the University of Utah Medical Center published a survey that detailed 246 risk factors related to coronary heart disease. Some were deemed to be of greater importance than others. Worldwide studies then set out to determine the *major* risk factors. We'll consider some of those studies and report on their conclusions.

The Framingham Heart Study

In 1951, the National Institute of Health initiated a study of the population of the town of Framingham, Massachusetts. The study deals with the way people live, eat, become ill, and die. Half of the middle-aged men and women in Framingham enrolled in the program when it started. Today the sons and daughters of the original participants have joined and are taking part in the research. This is the longest running, most comprehensive study of its kind in medical history.

Dr. William P. Castelli, the director of the Framingham Heart Study, reports that most of the heart attacks in Framingham occur in those people whose cholesterol levels are between 220 and 260. The average cholesterol of a Framingham coronary heart victim is 244.

Dr. Castelli wrote in the *American Journal of Forensic Medicine* in 1982 that the results of the following studies were all similar to the Framingham experience. The studies took place in Albany, among Minneapolis business executives, Peoples Gas Company employees in Chicago, Western Electric workers in Chicago, longshoremen in Los Angeles, and in Puerto Rico. All of these "within the population" studies showed the cause-and-effect relationship between cholesterol and CHD and heart attack; and between cholesterol and high blood pressure and stroke.

Dr. Castelli has made important observations about the relationship between cholesterol and CHD. For example, he says that in the thirty years of the Framingham study reseachers have never seen CHD in anyone whose cholesterol was 150 or lower. According to Dr. Castelli, "The evidence that people will do better if cholesterol is lowered is rather overwhelming. In every trial yet done, the people who lowered their cholesterol ran lowered risk of CHD."

Dr. Jeremiah Stamler of Northwestern University Medical School summarized the findings of many studies in these words, "The data is so massive that one can speak of the relationship [between cholesterol and CHD] as being beyond debate." He also states that studies over the past twenty-five years show a relationship between total fat in the diet, saturated fat, and CHD—the relationship we discussed earlier in the book as "cholesterol overload."

WHEN ARE YOU AT SERIOUS RISK?

A person is at serious risk today even if he has what once was considered a moderate cholesterol level. This fact was revealed at the 1985 annual meeting of the American Heart Association in a report on a study involving 356,222 men between the ages of thirty-five and fifty-seven. Researchers at twenty-five medical centers around the country measured and kept track of the cholesterol levels and blood pressure of all participants for six years. The study proved that risk factors increase alarmingly as cholesterol levels rise in men between the ages of forty and forty-four. The chart on page 36 shows the increase in risk until a man between forty and forty-four has a reading of 263 or above. At that point his CHD risk is five and a half times that of a man the same age with a cholesterol reading of 182.

THE CHD RISK IN MEN 40-44
AS CHOLESTEROL RISES

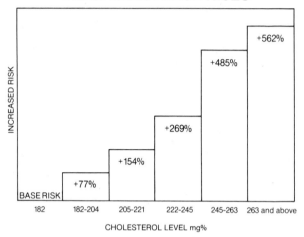

This chart proves the urgency of reducing your cholesterol immediately. We know you can do it! But first you should be aware of other factors contributing to CHD.

OTHER RISK INDICATORS

Cholesterol is the major cause of CHD in the sense that when it is present in the arteries in excessive amounts you are at higher risk. In that sense it might be more accurate to call cholesterol a risk "indicator." There are other factors or indicators that play a role in "causing" the cholesterol to be in your body in excessive and dangerous amounts. Understanding the factors can help you in your goal of halting and lowering cholesterol levels.

There Are Two Groups of Risk Factors

The two types of risk factors are unmodifiable (un-changeable) factors and modifiable (changeable) ones. Two factors that cannot be changed are gender and heredity.

Men are at far higher risk than women simply because of their sex. The mortality statistics show that men die in greater numbers and at an earlier age than women.

Heredity is the other unmodifiable risk factor; the role it plays in the disease has long been recognized. Dr. William Osler, who is frequently called the father of modern medicine, spoke of heredity this way, "Entire families sometimes show a tendency to early coronary atherosclerosis—a tendency which cannot be explained in any other way than that in the makeup of the machine, bad material was used for the tubing."

So if your father, mother, uncle, brother, or another close relative had a heart attack or died of CHD, your chances are well above average that the same thing can happen to you. (That is, if you don't take care of yourself now.)

Dr. Henry Blackburn, of the University of Minnesota School of Public Health, supports the theory that genetics determine a person's risk of coronary atherosclerosis. Blackburn says that the speed with which cholesterol deposits build up depends to a large degree on the genes. The hereditary factor would explain why some people develop coronary atherosclerosis and heart attacks at an early age, while other people are never in danger. In Dr. Blackburn's opinion, this problem has been around for years but it caused little trouble at a time in history when people subsisted on grains and vegetables. It has been only in the twentieth century, when Western populations began overloading their systems with a diet high in animal fats, that the genetic predisposition set off an epidemic of coronary atherosclerosis and heart attacks.

Even though heredity is unchangeable, there is growing evidence that by being more alert to risk factors, we can either control, undo, or alter some of the potential damage our genes have forecast.

Recently Johns Hopkins Hospital in Baltimore set up a center for preventive cardiology. The center's purpose is to cut the death toll from CHD by examining and helping people whose close relatives had a heart attack or a stroke before the age of sixty. These relatives of CHD victims are considered to be at high risk, and the aim of the center is to identify these people and give them counseling and treatment to reduce their risk. The program also teaches medical students and young physicians the importance of practicing preventive cardiology. Dr. Thomas Pearson, director of the Johns Hopkins Center, estimates that one half the annual mortality from CHD can be prevented.

Now let's deal with chronological age. Aging itself is *not* a risk factor; it is the degenerative diseases that occur more often when you get older that put you at risk. The older you get, the greater your risk of CHD. Annual mortality figures confirm this fact. But there is plenty of proof that by lowering your cholesterol you can lower your "cholesterol" biological age and so lower your risk for CHD no matter how old you are.

CHD Risk Factors You Can Change

The risk factors listed below can be changed, and all of them in one way or another are cholesterol-related.

1. High total blood cholesterol
2. Low HDL cholesterol levels
3. High blood pressure
4. Smoking
5. Lack of physical activity

High total blood cholesterol levels can be lowered quickly through changes in diet and life-style.

HDL cholesterol—the good cholesterol—can be increased through proper diet and increased physical activity. That is another benefit you gain from this program.

Because high blood pressure sometimes results when plaque creates blockages that slow the flow of blood and raise your blood pressure, this condition can be improved remarkably by diet, physical activity, and giving up smoking.

And what about smoking itself? We do not have a magic "stop smoking" program to give you. But if you smoke, the habit restricts your body's ability to cope with the excess cholesterol in your system. If you stop, your risk goes down.

We urge you to be active. If you live a sedentary life you don't gain the increase in HDL cholesterol that comes from a program of regular physical activity.

The accompanying chart shows how CHD risk for a fifty-year-old man increases with higher cholesterol levels, and the presence of risk factors that can be changed (some cholesterol-related, some not). Since you can change every one of those factors, doesn't it make good sense to start now to reduce your CHD risk?

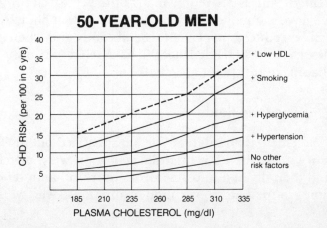

50-YEAR-OLD MEN

CHD RISK (per 100 in 6 yrs)

+ Low HDL
+ Smoking
+ Hyperglycemia
+ Hypertension
No other
risk factors

PLASMA CHOLESTEROL (mg/dl)

Risk Factors as CHD Predictors

Information about the presence and degree of one, some, or all of these conditions can help you predict the probability of CHD and heart attacks. That statement does not mean an absolutely certain prediction can be made for any single individual. It does mean, however, that predictions can be made about large segments of a population, and comparisons made between populations.

For example, the fact that you live in the United States makes it more likely you will have a heart attack than if you lived in another, less developed nation. This is true because the United States has one of the highest CHD rates in the world. The people of Japan, on the other hand, have a much lower average cholesterol level and a much lower rate of CHD. New information shows that in metropolitan Tokyo, where the Japanese have adopted a more Western diet that is high in saturated fats and cholesterol, CHD is on the increase.

THE PROOF THAT CHD CAN BE PREVENTED

Despite all this, let us emphasize that CHD *can* be prevented. This is proved by many of the research projects we have mentioned earlier. They show that cholesterol can be reduced quickly and significantly and when it is, deaths from CHD decline. We have selected two studies that make this point.

The Oslo Study

This was an intervention study carried out in Oslo, Norway. In it, 1,234 middle-aged men were matched and then divided into a control group and an intervention group. The intervention group (those who were to be encouraged to make changes in their diet and life-style) were given techniques designed to lower cholesterol through diet and techniques that would help them reduce or eliminate their smoking habit. The control group, on the other hand, continued to live as they did when the study began.

The Result: At the end of five years the incidence of fatal and nonfatal heart attacks and sudden death was 47 percent lower in the intervention group than in the control group. Researchers summarized the results by stating that receiving and acting upon information to improve diet and life-style is associated with significant risk reduction. The advice called for a sharp reduction in saturated fat in the diet and an increase in consumption of fruits, grains, legumes, and fresh vegetables.

These are the findings from another significant study:

The Zutphen Study

The purpose of this 1960 study was to investigate the relationship between fish consumption and CHD. A group of 852 middle-aged men from the town of Zutphen in the Netherlands were randomly selected for the study. Each participant, with the help of his wife, provided a careful history of his typical diet in the six to twelve months before the study. About 20 percent of the men did not eat any fish at all; others consumed on average anywhere from less than an ounce to over 10 ounces per day. The Zutphen men were followed for the next twenty years, during which time seventy-eight died of CHD.

The Result: A variety of scientific analyses proved an inverse relationship between fish consumption and CHD, meaning that the more fish eaten, the less the chance of developing CHD. Death from the disease was 50 percent lower among those who consumed a little over 1 ounce of fish daily than among those who did not eat fish at all. The researchers concluded that as little as one or two fish dishes per week may serve as an excellent preventive measure against heart disease.

Now that it is clear that the right diet and life-style is beneficial in reducing CHD, the question is, should *you* change your diet?

ARE YOU A CANDIDATE FOR CHD?

The answer is *Yes* if you fall into one or more of these categories.

1. If you're over thirty years of age and your cholesterol is over 170, you should take immediate steps to reduce your risk.

2. After the age of fifty the risk of CHD becomes greater for both men and women. So practically everyone over fifty should examine their diet and life-style and make the appropriate changes recommended in this book.

3. If your blood pressure is high (over 140/80), you should immediately reduce your risk factors.

4. Regardless of your gender, if you are ten pounds or more overweight you should apply the Bio-Nutrionics nutrition approach to risk-factor reduction.

5. Women approaching menopause should consider risk-factor reduction.

It was from Dr. Castelli that we learned that women are protected somehow from coronary heart disease prior to menopause. In the Framingham study only six out of 1,600 premenopausal women developed CHD. But after menopause women catch up with the male rate of death and the curves for CHD deaths in men and women eventually join.

EVERYONE SHOULD THINK ABOUT REDUCING HIS OR HER RISK

Dr. Thomas E. Kottke, of the University of Minnesota School of Cardiology, says that everyone should reduce their risk to coronary heart disease. We concur whole-heartedly. As mortality statistics now stand, half of us will die of CHD. The important fact to remember is that coronary heart disease is exactly that—a disease. It can be prevented. Most important, *it is not a natural part of the aging process*. Evidence of the disease has been found in autopsy reports of children as young as two or three years old who died from accidental causes. Now is the time to prepare yourself for better health.

BIO-NUTRIONICS: THE GOOD NEWS

Despite the prevalence of CHD in America, cardiac mortality rates have declined 2 percent to 3 percent each year over the past fifteen years. We believe that millions of Americans finally have accepted the relationship between CHD, diet, and life-style. They no longer believe advances in medications, new emergency techniques, improved facilities, and advanced medical care are the only answers to the problem. Americans have made real changes in their eating habits and activity programs, and the downward trend in CHD deaths is evident in all age, sex, and ethnic groups in the entire adult population in all regions of the country. Most important, the rate of decline of the disease is greater in the United States than in any other country in the world.

So if you are one of the people who is set to actively take charge of your health, read on. In the chapters that follow we will present "the good news": an easy-to-follow "wellness" program that promises to reduce your high cholesterol and ultimately make you feel great.

3. The Bio-Nutrionics Program to Cholesterol Reduction

Bio-Nutrionics is a completely unique nutrition and life-style plan that incorporates most of the methods that have been learned in the past twenty-five years of research for reducing cholesterol. It is effective for men and women of all ages, is safe and easy to follow, and will give you results in thirty days or less.

YOUR PERSONAL RISK ANALYSIS
QUESTIONNAIRE

Begin the program with our personal risk factor questionnaire which begins on page 47. It asks you for your appraisal of your current diet and life-style. For the sake of your health, please be honest and forthright in your answers. No one except you will see them unless you wish to show the questionnaire to your doctor, a friend, or family member for discussion of the program. Your answers will help you judge if you're at risk now, and whether after thirty days on the program you have succeeded in reducing your CHD risk factors.

Self-scoring tests like the one you are about to take have proven to be valuable as a public health tool, because they help people understand health problems and encourage individual efforts to improve health. This questionnaire is based on information from a number of sources including the Framingham Heart Study, Dr. Peter Wood, Dr. Alan Dyer, Dr. Jeremiah Stamler, and Dr. Phyllis Pirie. Dr. Pirie has been credited with validating a self-scoring test for coronary heart disease risks. It has been established scientifically that this type of questionnaire is an accurate tool for assessing a person's risk and reduction of risk over a period of time.

It is, however, important to point out that there is no way a questionnaire can be used to measure specific cholesterol values. These can be measured only with a blood test. If you have had a physical examination recently you might wish to get the results of your cholesterol reading from your doctor and enter that figure at the beginning of the questionnaire. Also ask your doctor for your blood-pressure reading and enter that as well. For the most accurate comparison of your results at the conclusion of thirty days, you may wish to obtain new cholesterol and blood-pressure readings from your doctor or a medical laboratory.

Begin our questionnaire by entering your answers to the twelve questions in the column headed "Start of Program." The questions deal with weight, blood pressure, physical activity, blood sugar, stress, and diet. Each question is numbered. You have a choice of answers listed under each question. Each is given a "point value" which is listed under the column labeled "Point Value." Read each answer carefully and then select the one that best describes your condition. Make sure you select only

one answer to each question and be sure you enter the
plus sign or minus sign in front of the point value when
you enter it in the "Start of the Program" column. When
you are done, add up the total of plus and minus points
and enter that total as "your total score" at the end of
the questionnaire.

Personal Risk Factor Questionnaire

	Point Value	Start of Program	After 30 Days
1. Weight			
A. Underweight or normal	0	_____	_____
B. Overweight with no weight loss in last thirty days	+10	_____	_____
C. Overweight with loss of 3 pounds or more in last thirty days	+5	_____	_____
2. Blood Pressure			
A. Blood pressure normal (140/80 or lower) or you are taking blood-pressure medications	0	_____	_____
B. Blood pressure high (over 140/80). Not taking medication and your blood pressure has not come down in the last thirty days	+10	_____	_____
C. Blood pressure high (over 140/80). Not taking medication, but your blood			

	Point Value	Start of Program	After 30 Days
pressure has come down significantly in the last thirty days	+5	_____	_____
3. Exercise			
A. No *regular* exercise (less than five times per week)	+10	_____	_____
B. Mild exercise equal to walking half an hour a day at least five times a week	−5	_____	_____
C. Aerobic exercise at least twenty minutes four times per week	−15	_____	_____
4. Blood Sugar			
A. Have you ever been told that your blood sugar is too high (greater than 130 mg/dl)?	+10	_____	_____
B. Blood sugar is normal	0	_____	_____
C. Do not know if blood sugar is normal	0	_____	_____
5. Smoking Habits			
A. Currently smoke a pipe or cigar	+5	_____	_____
B. Smoke less than one pack of cigarettes a day	+5	_____	_____
C. Smoke more than one pack of cigarettes a day	+10	_____	_____

	Point Value	Start of Program	After 30 Days
D. Do not smoke now but have smoked in the last year	0	_____	_____
E. Never smoked, or used to smoke but have not smoked in the last year	−5	_____	_____
6. Stress			
A. I am "high-strung" and react strongly to stressful situations (type A behavior)	+5	_____	_____
B. Sometimes I'm "high-strung" and sometimes I'm calm	0	_____	_____
C. I am basically a calm person and do not react to stressful situations in an extreme manner	−5	_____	_____
7. Dietary Fat Consumption (red meats, fried and fatty foods, eggs and dairy products)			
A. Above average	+10	_____	_____
B. Average	+5	_____	_____
C. Below average	−10	_____	_____
8. Vegetable Consumption			
A. Above average	−5	_____	_____
B. Average	+5	_____	_____
C. Below average	+10	_____	_____
9. Consumption of Unprocessed Cereal Grains (brown rice and whole-wheat products)			

	Point Value	Start of Program	After 30 Days
A. Above average	−5	_____	_____
B. Average	+5	_____	_____
C. Below average	+10	_____	_____

10. Consumption of Refined Sugar in Foods such as Soft Drinks, Candies and Pastries

A. Above average	+10	_____	_____
B. Average	+5	_____	_____
C. Below average	0	_____	_____

11. Consumption of fried foods and packaged foods containing "hydrogenated oil" such as potato chips, breaded and fried chicken or fish, and margarine is:

A. Above average	+10	_____	_____
B. Average	+5	_____	_____
C. Below average	−5	_____	_____

12. Are you currently engaged in a program to change your lifestyle (including nutritional and exercise components) in order to reduce your risk of CHD?

A. Yes	−10	_____	_____
B. No	0	_____	_____

YOUR TOTAL SCORE	_____	_____

Now check the chart below to discover your current state of health.

If your number is	Your risk level is
−31 to −60	extremely low
0 to −30	low
+1 to +30	moderate
+31 to +60	high
+61 and above	extremely high

At the end of the first month, retake the questionnaire, filling out the column headed "After 30 Days." At that time add up and compare your total with the one you had before starting the program. The numbers will tell you immediately how well you're progressing. And if you are following our plan seriously, we guarantee you will move into a risk category at least one level lower than when you first began Bio-Nutrionics.

GETTING MOTIVATED

Remember, no matter how low your score, there is still room to improve your health and reduce your cholesterol. Don't despair! By following our program, you'll see and feel results faster than you expect. The recommendations we make will help fend off depression, too. Perhaps this is because once you make the decision to improve your body, your mental outlook automatically improves in the process. We see this happen all the time.

We realize that making any changes in lifelong eating and activity habits can be difficult. We're behind you all the way. Just determine to do something lasting for yourself. It will help your self-image and when we perceive ourselves as healthy and energetic, others view us that way, too. This attitude can go a long way toward improving your self-esteem.

Your reason for starting the program may be for wanting to prolong your life for the good of your loved ones. Whatever the reason, it's time to get on the mark, get set, and go!

HOW THE PROGRAM WORKS

1. The program is based on six carefully selected, easy-to-follow food lists that help you plan healthful, nutritious meals. And although calories count, *you will not have to count calories because the food lists furnish you with portioned servings.*

2. The key to using the food lists to plan your daily menus is knowing your recommended weight. You can determine it by following the instructions and using the chart on pages 67 and 68.

3. The program includes seventy-one recipes for delicious dishes that are low in cholesterol, fats, and calories. You also will learn tips on food shopping, menu planning, and eating out.

4. Important information is offered on the place of vitamin and mineral supplements in your eating plan.

5. Because dietary changes are only one way of lowering cholesterol, the program concludes with an unstrenuous physical activity plan geared to fit your lifestyle.

SMOKING

If you stop smoking *now* you begin reducing risk factors immediately. We mention smoking here because it is the only habit discussed in your questionnaire that cannot be modified by altering diet or exercise. It is a life-style change you must be responsible for. Stopping smoking will reduce your risk of CHD to a greater degree than any other single change!

Smokers have three times the risk of nonfatal heart attacks as nonsmokers. Additionally, a smoker who has a heart attack is three times more likely to die of sudden cardiac death than a nonsmoker.

The most recent research indicates that in two years after stopping smoking, an ex-smoker's risk is identical to that of a nonsmoker.

The nicotine and the carbon monoxide in cigarettes are damaging. Nicotine irritates the heart muscle, increases the heart rate, shrinks the arteries, and increases blood pressure. If your blood pressure is high and you stop smoking, chances are your blood pressure will start to go down without medication even before you make major changes in your diet. Finally, the carbon monoxide in the cigarette smoke reduces the supply of oxygen to your heart.

According to one authority, heavy smokers subject themselves to eight times the carbon monoxide levels allowed by industry. Without question, smokers have a far higher risk of developing chronic bronchitis, emphysema, and lung cancer as well as CHD. These facts led one researcher to state recently that few medical interventions can provide such rapid and substantial benefits with so little expense and so few side effects as giving up smoking. By quitting you will improve your health immeasurably and save money.

We hope that you stop smoking because if you do your efforts will be doubly rewarding.

4. The Nutrition Plan

One of the most important elements of the Bio-Nutrionics Program is its Nutrition Plan. Although it requires some changes in your eating habits, we guarantee you'll be able to eat the foods you like, but in the right combinations. There are enough selections in our food lists to satisfy even the most finicky eater. As we mentioned in the Introduction, Bio-Nutrionics recognizes and encourages individual food preferences. The eating plan has been designed to be flexible and appealing. We know you'll have no trouble sticking with it. Follow it and your body will function better, serve you better, and afford you more stamina and energy.

FOODS TO EAT AND FOODS TO AVOID

In the diagrams on page 56, you will see a comparison of the typical American diet and the Bio-Nutrionics Plan. They show you visually the difference between how you now eat and a more healthful way of eating.

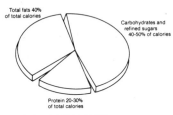

TYPICAL AMERICAN DIET

Total fats 40% of total calories

Carbohydrates and refined sugars 40-50% of calories

Protein 20-30% of total calories

1. Excessively high in total fats.
2. Very low in complex carbohydrates.
3. High in refined sugars.
4. Very high in protein.

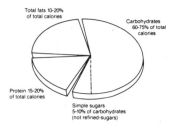

BIO-NUTRIONICS NUTRITION PLAN

Total fats 10-20% of total calories

Carbohydrates 60-75% of total calories

Protein 15-20% of total calories

Simple sugars 5-10% of carbohydrates (not refined-sugars)

1. Sharply reduced fat consumption.
2. Increased intake of complex carbohydrates, grains, legumes and whole foods.
3. Sharply reduced consumption of refined sugars.
4. Moderately reduced consumption of protein.

Listed below is a summary of those changes:

1. Sharply reduce your intake of foods high in saturated fats.

2. Double your consumption of complex carbohydrates, including foods high in fiber.

3. Satisfy your craving for sweets with fruits and other naturally sweet foods.

4. Limit red meat to three times a week in portions up to 4 ounces after cooking, and limit eggs to a total of six per week.

5. Reduce the amount of dairy products that you normally eat.

Again, the items we ask you to limit will be replaced by healthy, tasty treats. There is nothing bland about the foods in the plan. Corn on the cob, nuts, popcorn, beef, potatoes, wine, and frozen yogurt can all be eaten without a bit of guilt.

THE FATS IN OUR DIET

To reduce high blood cholesterol the Nutrition Plan calls for an immediate sharp reduction in dietary fats.

The American diet is bubbling over with fats of all kinds. On average, Americans consume over 40 percent of their dietary calories in fats. It is estimated that the amount of fat in the average American diet has increased by one pound per year for the past thirty-five years.

A great deal of the fat people consume can't be seen. Even when it is cut from a piece of meat, 15 percent of the trimmed, apparently lean meat is invisible fat.

We are surrounded by temptations. Pelted with food advertisements, we indulge too often in fast-food cheeseburgers that pack over 1,000 calories apiece, a good deal of it fat. The cheese on the burger is filled with saturated fat—the worst kind. And who can resist french fries that always seem to go with the hamburger? You can bet they've been cooked in hydrogenated fat, a dangerous, man-made variety.

Not All Fats Are Bad

Let's learn the difference between the undesirable fats and the desirable fats.

Saturated Fats, the Undesirable Fat: These are the fats that come from animal sources. Saturated fats are typically solid at room temperature. Lard, butter, and animal meat contain lots of saturated fat. Saturated fats increase the LDL (low-density lipoproteins) in the blood. These are the fats that contribute to cholesterol overload. (For a discussion of LDLs, see page 27).

Unsaturated Fats, the Desirable Fat: These fats are usually liquid at room temperature. There are two classifications of unsaturated fats that are distinguishable from each other by their chemical makeup. For our purposes we need to know that one type is monounsaturated fat, like olive oil, while the other is polyunsaturated fat, often identified as PUFA. Both are beneficial and allowable in the eating plan.

The most common and outstanding monounsaturated fat you are likely to encounter is olive oil. It is the one recommended for cooking and as a salad oil. When buying it for salad dressing ask for virgin olive oil. Its flavor can't be beat.

Polyunsaturated fats fall into two groups that have different molecular structures. The first is called the Omega-6 group. Corn, sunflower, sesame, and safflower oils and other vegetable oils that are commonly used are high in Omega-6 components.

The second group of polyunsaturated fats are known as Omega-3. Recent findings have brought the Omega-3 oils into prominence. They are the cold-weather fish oils that are found in haddock, cod, and mackerel. The oils of walnuts, hazelnuts, soybeans, and the flax plant (linseed oil) are also high in Omega-3 components.

The Omega-3 and Omega-6 oils are called essential fatty acids (EFAs), the fatty acids the body itself cannot produce and which are required for good health.

Dr. Donald Rudin, a leading authority in Omega-3 research, says that Americans are 80 percent depleted of Omega-3 oils. They have been systematically taken out of the diet because of their tendency to become rancid quickly. Dr. Rudin is a leader in the effort to reintroduce linseed oil back into the average diet. This oil from the flax plant, which is 50 percent Omega-3, was a traditional cooking oil in Northern Europe prior to World War II. In the Ukraine, it was delivered to homes fresh daily. Linseed oil is a valuable addition to your diet because your body converts it to the same oils found in fish.

Research into the Omega-3 oils has demonstrated that they have a remarkable ability to lower lipid levels in the blood. As a result, the blood flows more freely and blood pressure is lowered. Can't beat those benefits, can you?

The research into Omega-3 oils was inspired by remarkable stories of the native Eskimo population of Greenland. It was recognized that these Eskimos, living almost exclusively on a fish diet, have "safe" cholesterol levels, low levels of triglycerides (the main fat found in the body), prolonged bleeding time (meaning they have thinner blood that is less likely to clot and block arteries), and *they have little heart disease.*

The lesson learned is to increase the amount of fish you consume and add the oil of the flax plant, namely linseed oil, to your diet. Please be sure, when purchasing linseed oil, that you get the food-grade oil from your health-food store or supermarket, and *not* the type sold in hardware stores.

Dangerous Man-made Fats: A dangerous, man-made group of fats is created when unsaturated fats are hydrogenated by adding the chemical hydrogen to an oil. The molecular structure of the oil is changed in a way that keeps it from becoming rancid and gives it longer shelf life.

If the words "hydrogenated" or "partially hydrogenated" appear on the label, avoid using the product. Here in the United States we consume hydrogenated fats in great quantities because they are the oils used for deep frying fish, chicken, and potatoes. Hydrogenated fats are consumed in huge quantities in Germany and Poland, two more examples of nations with heart attack epidemics. In those countries where hydrogenated fats are seldom used and where animal fat consumption is minimal coronary artery disease death rates are low. These countries include: Spain, Greece, Italy, Yugoslavia, Bulgaria, and Rumania.

Which Fat Is Best for Cooking?

The best all-around oil for cooking is olive oil. It is stable at higher temperatures and does not "oxidize," or become rancid, easily. The polyunsaturated oils are not to be used for cooking. They oxidize when heated and should be used "cold" as in salad dressings.

Regardless of which oil you use, please remember that deep frying of any kind should be avoided.

AVOID FOODS THAT ARE PROCESSED AND CONTAIN REFINED SUGAR

The Bio-Nutrionics Program emphasizes foods that are natural, whole, and unprocessed. That's the way nature "packages" nutrients and that's the way we believe they should be consumed.

Food manufacturers or producers sometimes preserve their products with chemical additives to prolong their shelf life. Before buying foods, read the labels; if you cannot pronounce the ingredients, don't purchase the product.

Foods that are processed or refined have been literally taken apart and then put back together. All the valuable nutrients are not put back in. Although the word "refined" may appeal to some consumers and advertisers, a more appropriate term is "stripped." For example, in the process of making white flour, the fiber and bran portion of wheat is separated and discarded from the kernel. The resulting white "flour" is a plain starch that has very little nutritional value other than calories.

When we talk about sweets, we should be aware that there are refined sugars and unrefined sugars. The refined sugars are simple sugars which have been stripped of all other nutrients, unlike the unrefined sugars in fruits, which nature packages along with fiber, vitamins, and minerals. So we ask you to avoid refined sugars such as those found in candy and soda pop. The energy burst you get from refined sugar (like chocolate) is only temporary. If you have a craving for sweets, eat a piece of fruit or try one of the desserts in our recipe section for an after-dinner treat.

FIBER IN OUR DIET: WHAT IT IS, WHAT IT DOES, AND WHY WE NEED IT

Anyone who watches television commercials knows that manufacturers are pushing cereals containing fiber. Similarly, many of you may recall a parent or grandparent who urged you to eat more fiber. They were right.

What is fiber? It is the undigestible portion of food which is not absorbed by our bodies. It is a substance that promotes regularity, stabilizes blood-sugar levels, and lessens the risk of heart disease and colon cancer. Bran, apples, all grains—including brown rice—and green vegetables all contain significant amounts of fiber. Yet be alert that some fibers outperform others. One is oat bran, a delicious hot cereal that nutritionists believe can reduce cholesterol levels with surprising speed. One cup of oat bran as a daily breakfast cereal can reduce low-density lipoproteins in a single month by 10 percent in some individuals. Anyone with high cholesterol should consider this approach along with the rest of the program to lower cholesterol and increase stamina.

Americans suffer from a number of conditions as a result of insufficient fiber in their diet, conditions virtually unknown in other parts of the world. In Africa, as an example, heart disease is almost nonexistent. Its incidence is just beginning to increase slowly in large cities. Also unknown in Africa is diverticular disease, the most common disease of the colon in the United States. It can be found here in nearly half the American population over the age of fifty. Cancers of the colon and rectum are also rare among Africans, but they are leading causes of death in our culture.

Fiber has been largely neglected because its nature has been misunderstood and its important role in maintaining normal gastrointestinal function has not been appreciated. Simply put, fiber helps our intestinal tract work properly.

While it's true that as a nation we are consuming more fruits and vegetable fiber, these sources apparently have much less effect on bowel physiology than does cereal fiber. We ask you to consume oat bran or any high-fiber cereal at breakfast.

PLAN YOUR DAILY MEALS FROM SIX FOOD GROUPS

You'll be eating a recommended number of daily servings from each of six food groups that are listed on page 66. By doing this you will enjoy healthy, balanced, nutritious meals every day.

Food Group 1: The Mineral Vegetables

Dark green leafy vegetables like spinach, kale, lettuce, and broccoli are high in minerals, such as magnesium and potassium (which effect blood-pressure regulation) and calcium (which helps prevent osteoporosis). Magnesium is contained in the green coloring matter of plants called chlorophyll. Chlorophyll is similar to the hemoglobin in our blood. As a matter of fact, chlorophyll and hemoglobin are almost identical except that chlorophyll contains magnesium and hemoglobin contains iron.

We know from both scientific study and general knowledge that people living on vegetarian diets have far lower risk factors for CHD. For example, Dr. Mildred S. Seelig, in her book *Magnesium Deficiency in the Pathogenesis of Disease*, has established that an overabundance of dietary fat interferes with the absorption of magnesium in the body, and that magnesium deficiencies are an indicator, or risk factor, for CHD. Likewise, Seventh Day Adventists, who are practicing vegetarians, on average live seven years longer than the average American. Dr. William Castelli of the Framingham Study has stressed that vegetarians have very low cholesterol levels, and Dr. Frank Sacks of the Harvard Medical School has studied the vegetarian community and has come to the following conclusion: Strict vegetarians who consumed dairy products on an average of three times a month and meat less than seven times a year maintained cholesterol levels in the 125–145 range. We are not necessarily suggesting that you become a vegetarian, but we are emphasizing the health-promoting benefits of vegetables high in minerals. The accompanying chart shows the high mineral content of three of the most nutritious green vegetables in comparison with beef, bacon, and Big Macs.

Nutrients per 100 Calories
(mg = milligrams)

	Spinach	Kale	Broccoli	Beef	Bacon	Big Mac
Calcium	358 mg	471 mg	322 mg	3 mg	8 mg	28 mg
Magnesium	338 mg	97 mg	75 mg	8 mg	2 mg	6 mg
Potassium	1808 mg	837 mg	1191 mg	117 mg	46 mg	43 mg
Iron	11.9 mg	5.8 mg	3.4 mg	0.9 mg	0.9 mg	0.7 mg
Fat	1.2 g	2.1 g	0.9 g	8.6 g	10.4 g	5.9 g

Food Group 2: Grains and Carbohydrate Vegetables

Carbohydrate food will make up as much as 60 to 75 percent of your Nutrition Plan. The largest portion of your carbohydrate intake will be from food list 2. This list contains food from plant sources that are high in fiber and high in starch, known as complex carbohydrates. Whole grains are included in this food group. They are one of nature's finest sources of complex carbohydrates. Wheat, barley, oats, corn, brown rice, and buckwheat groats (known as kasha) are to be found here. Recipes in Chapter 5 offer many delicious ways to prepare and serve the grains and vegetables in food group 2.

Food Group 3: Fruits

These are unrefined simple carbohydrates and will make up between 5 percent and 10 percent of your total carbohydrate food consumption. By eating the recommended daily servings of fruit you will be able to sharply reduce your intake of refined sugar. Fruits rank high on our list of whole foods. They are packaged in their own protective skins and modern transportation has made it possible for us to enjoy exotic fresh fruits from all over the world almost year round. Nothing, of course, can surpass fresh-picked fruit right out of your own backyard or from your nearest farmer's market. Eat the whole fruit in preference to drinking fruit juices whenever you can. It is high in pectin, a fiber that aids digestion. Fruit will maintain your energy level and satisfy your hunger between meals.

Food Group 4: Dairy Foods

We urge you to stay well within the guidelines in this food group. It is very easy to increase your saturated fat intake with dairy foods, so be careful. Be sure to purchase cheese made from part-skim milk or low-fat milk. The hard cheeses like Parmesan are the best because they provide a lot of flavor in a small serving. The best food in this group is active yogurt because it replenishes the beneficial bacteria, lactobacillus, in your intestines. Be sure to buy plain active-culture low-fat yogurt.

Food Group 5: Protein

You will be eating far less protein than is found in the typical American diet. Most of us eat high-protein diets in the mistaken notion that protein is a high-energy food. Top athletes once ate steak dinners before big events to give them extra strength and vitality—but not anymore. Sports nutritionists have found that complex carbohydrates are better. They are nature's "time release" energy food because they are metabolized over a period of time, and today's athletic hero is more likely to put away a huge plate of pasta rather than a steak just before game time.

Protein is important for growth, maintaining body tissue, regulating water balance, and forming essential body compounds. But excess protein does increase the risk of osteoporosis.

Food Group 6: Desserts, Snacks, Condiments, and Beverages

This food list is filled with delicious, nutritious treats like nuts, which are a rich source of nutrients. But make sure you buy unsalted nuts and stop eating them before you exceed the recommended limits. This section also puts alcoholic beverages in perspective. Our common-sense position is that alcohol is generally more harmful to the body than it is beneficial. We also feel that the term "moderate" when applied to drinking alcohol can be stretched to mean anything from a glass of wine with dinner to a three-martini lunch. Common sense also tells us this is no place for a temperance lecture. It is unrealistic to expect even a moderate drinker to become a nondrinker overnight. But we urge you to count your drinks just as you do the food on the food list—and count every one. Alcohol may result in increased blood fat (triglycerides), as well as depleting the body of essential vitamins and minerals. Our strongest recommendation is that you limit your intake of liquor, wine, or beer to two servings a day at the very most.

We suggest that you also use this food list as a guide to between-meal snacks that may replace the danish and the candy bar that many of us eat from time to time— more out of habit than desire.

CALORIES COUNT—BUT YOU DON'T HAVE TO COUNT THEM

You may wish to know the number of calories in a serving in each food group so they are listed below:

Food Group	Calories per serving
1. Mineral Vegetables	50
2. Grains and Carbohydrate Vegetables	100
3. Fruits	50
4. Dairy	100
5. Protein	50
6. Desserts, Snacks, Beverages	100

We have used these calorie values per serving to make sure you are eating the correct number of portioned servings from each food list according to the weight recommended for your height and body build. *You simply count servings, NOT CALORIES.*

How to Find Your Recommended Weight and Plan Your Daily Menus

Below and on page 68 you will find charts of recommended weights for men and women. Decide whether you are a person of small frame, medium frame, or large frame. Run your finger down the chart until you find your height, then move across until you come to the correct frame size. (A man 5'10" tall of medium frame will have a recommended weight of 155, and a woman 5'6" tall of small frame has a recommended weight of 125 pounds.)

Men
Recommended Weight for Your Height and Build*

Height		Small Frame	Medium Frame	Large Frame
Feet	Inches			
5	2	130	135	145
5	3	135	135	145
5	4	135	140	150
5	5	135	140	150
5	6	140	145	155
5	7	140	150	155
5	8	145	150	160
5	9	145	155	165
5	10	150	155	165
5	11	150	160	170
6	0	155	165	175
6	1	155	165	180
6	2	160	170	185
6	3	165	175	190
6	4	170	180	195

*The men's chart includes 5 pounds of clothing to be worn when stepping on the scale.

Women
Recommended Weight for Your Height and Build*

Height				
Feet	*Inches*	*Small Frame*	*Medium Frame*	*Large Frame*
4	10	105	115	125
4	11	110	120	125
5	0	110	120	130
5	1	115	125	130
5	2	115	125	130
5	3	120	130	140
5	4	120	130	140
5	5	125	135	145
5	6	125	135	150
5	7	130	140	150
5	8	130	140	155
5	9	135	145	160
5	10	140	145	160
5	11	140	145	165
6	0	145	155	165

*The women's chart includes 3 pounds of clothing and 1″ in height for low heels worn when stepping on the scale.

Now that you have found your recommended weight move right along to the charts on the following pages. There's one for men and one for women. Please make sure you use the correct chart.

Run your finger down the recommended-weight column on the left and you will find in the columns to the right of your weight the number of recommended daily servings you should eat in each of the six food groups.

Now we'll apply the same examples we previously used in finding recommended weights and we learn:

Our 5′10″ man of medium frame with a recommended weight of 155 pounds will select 155 as his guide. His daily food list will be:

Food Group 1: 6 servings

Food Group 2: 6 servings
Food Group 3: 3 servings
Food Group 4: 2 servings
Food Group 5: 6 servings
Food Group 6: 3 servings

Our 5'6" woman of small frame with a recommended weight of 125 pounds will select 125 as her guide. Her daily food list will be:

Food Group 1: 6 servings
Food Group 2: 4 servings
Food Group 3: 2 servings
Food Group 4: 1 serving
Food Group 5: 5 servings
Food Group 6: 2 servings

On pages 82 and 83 immediately following the food lists we will show you how our 5'6" woman used the food lists to plan her meals for a day.

Men
Recommended Number of Portions to Eat Per Day in Each Food Group
The portions have been determined by your recommended weight shown in the left-hand column.

Recommended Weight	1 Mineral Vegetables	2 Grains and Carbohydrate Vegetables	3 Fruit	4 Dairy	5 Protein	6 Desserts, Snacks, Beverages
120	6	5	2	1	5	2
125	6	5	2	1	6	2
130	6	5	2–3	1	6	2
135	6	5–6	3	1	6	2
140	6	6	3	1	6	2
145	6	6	3	1–2	6	2

Recommended Weight	1 Mineral Vegetables	2 Grains and Carbohydrate Vegetables	3 Fruit	4 Dairy	5 Protein	6 Desserts, Snacks, Beverages
150	6	6	3	2	6	2
155	6	6	3	2	6	2–3
160	6	6	3	2	6	3
165	6	6	3	2	7	3
170	7	6	3	2	7	3
175	7	6–7	3	2	7	3
180	7	7	3	2	7	3
185	7	7	3	2	7	3–4
190	7	7	3	2	7	4
195	7	7	3	2	8	4
200	8	7	3	2	8	4
205	8	7–8	3	2	8	4
210	8	8	3	2	8	4
215	8	8	4	2	8	4
220	8	8	4	2	8	4–5
225	8	8	4	2	8	5
230	8	8	5	2	8	5
235	8	8–9	5	2	8	5
240	8	9	5	2	8	5
245	8	9–10	5	2	8	5
250	8	10	5	2	8	5

Women
Recommended Number of Portions to Eat Per Day in Each Food Group

The portions have been determined by your recommended weight shown in the left-hand column.

Recommended Weight	1 Minerals Vegetables	2 Grains and Carbohydrate Vegetables	3 Fruit	4 Dairy	5 Protein	6 Desserts, Snacks, Beverages
90	4–5	3	2	1	4	1
95	5	3	2	1	4	1
100	5	3–4	2	1	4	1
105	5	4	2	1	4	1

Recommended Weight	1 Minerals Vegetables	2 Grains and Carbohydrate Vegetables	3 Fruit	4 Dairy	5 Protein	6 Desserts, Snacks, Beverages
110	5	4	2	1	4	1–2
115	5	4	2	1	4	2
120	5	4	2	1	5	2
125	6	4	2	1	5	2
130	6	4–5	2	1	5	2
135	6	5	2	1	5	2
140	6	5	2	1	5–6	2
145	6	5	2–3	1	6	2
150	6	5	3	1	6	2
155	6	5–6	3	1	6	2
160	6	6	3	1	6	2
165	6	6	3	1–2	6	2
170	6	6	3	2	6	2
175	6	6	3	2	6	2–3
180	6	6	3	2	6	3

Food Group 1: Mineral Vegetables

Each 1-cup serving provides 50 calories unless noted otherwise in the list below.

Artichoke
Asparagus
Bamboo shoots
Beet greens
Beets
Broccoli
Brussels sprouts
Cabbage
Carrot greens
Carrots
Cauliflower

Celery
Chard
Collard greens
Cucumber
Dandelion greens
Eggplant
Green sweet peppers
Kale
Kelp
Kohlrabi
Mushrooms
Mustard greens
Okra
Onions
Parsley
Peppers
Radishes
Red cabbage
Rhubarb
Romaine lettuce (and other dark-green leafy lettuce)
Scallions
Soups (noncreamed, vegetable only)
Spinach
Sprouts
String beans
Summer squash
Swiss chard
Tomato sauce ($\frac{1}{3}$ cup)
Tomatoes
Turnip greens
All vegetable juices
Water chestnuts
Watercress
Zucchini

NOTE: One serving of salad should equal 2 cups (2 portions). So by having a salad for both lunch and dinner you are eating 4 daily portions of mineral vegetables. You are also eating whole foods that are uncooked, so they have retained the greatest part of their vitamin and mineral content. We suggest that you shop the farmer's markets where growers are selling direct to consumers. You'll discover fresher foods, fresher vegetables in season, and a variety of better quality items at lower prices than those offered in grocery stores and supermarkets.

Food Group 2: Grains and Carbohydrate Vegetables

Each 1-cup serving provides 100 calories unless noted otherwise in the list below.

1 6-inch round tortilla
Barley, ½ cup
Beans, ½ cup
Blackeyed peas, ½ cup
Bran muffin, ⅓ muffin (1 ounce)
Brown rice, ½ cup
Buckwheat, ½ cup
Bulgur, ½ cup
Cassava
Cold cereal, 1 ounce
Cornbread, 2 × 2-inch square
Corn flour, ¼ cup
Cornmeal, ½ cup
Corn muffin, ⅓ muffin (1 ounce)
Corn on cob, 1 small
Crackers, 4
Dried peas or beans, ½ cup

English muffin, ½
Frijoles (beans), 3 ounces
Garbanzo beans (chick-peas), ½ cup
Granola (made without butter or oil), ½ cup
Green peas (fresh), 1 cup
Grits, ⅔ cup
Hot cereal
Jicama
Kasha (made with little or no oil)
Kidney beans, ½ cup
Lentils, ½ cup
Lima beans, ½ cup
Millet, ½ cup
Mung beans, ½ cup
Nacho chips, 10 chips
Navy beans, ½ cup
Oatmeal, ¾ cup
Parsnips
Pasta, ½ cup (whole-grain, artichoke, spinach)
Pinto beans, ½ cup
Plantain
Popcorn (air-popped), 1 quart
Potato flour, ⅓ cup
Pumpkin
Red beans, ½ cup
Rice cakes, 3
Rice flour, ¼ cup
Rutabaga
Rye berries
Rye flour, ¼ cup
Sorghum, 1 cup
Soups, ¾ cup (meatless, noncreamed bean, and legumes)
Soybeans, ½ cup
Soybean flour, ½ cup

Spaghetti squash
Succotash, ½ cup
Sweet potato, ⅓ cup
Taco shells, 2 small
Tortilla flour, 1 ounce
Triticale
Wheat berries
White potato, 1 medium (with skin)
Whole-grain bread, 1 slice
Whole-wheat bagel, ½
Whole-wheat bread, 1 slice
Whole-wheat pita bread, 1 pocket (1½ ounce)
Whole-wheat roll, 1 small
Wild rice, ¾ cup
Winter squash
Yams, ½ cup
Yellow rose potato, 1 small

NOTE: Don't believe what you may have heard about pasta being fattening. It's the heavy, oily sauces many people use on pasta that have given it that reputation. Use the sauces in the recipe section of Chapter 5 on pasta dishes, and remember that a large dish of pasta (2 cups) uses 2 of your daily grain and carbohydrate portions. It is commonly thought that potatoes, a starch like pasta, also are fattening—but that's not true either. Add variety to your diet with grits, kasha, an assortment of beans, and the flavor of vegetables like parsnips and rutabaga.

Food Group 3: Fruits

Each serving provides about 50 calories and the serving size is noted next to each fruit listed below.

Apple, 1 small
Apple juice, ½ cup

Applesauce (unsweetened), ½ cup
Banana, ½
Black currants (raw), ¾ cup
Blackberries, ½ cup
Blueberries, ½ cup
Cantaloupe, ⅓ small melon
Carambola, 1 small
Casaba melon, 2-inch wedge
Cherimoya, 2 ounces
Cherries, 10
Coconut (fresh), ½ ounce
Cranberries (raw), 1 cup
Cranberry sauce, ¼ cup
Dates, 2
Dried apricots, 5 halves
Dried figs, 1
Dried fruit, 2 pieces
Fresh apricots, 3
Fresh figs, 2
Fresh orange juice, ½ cup
Fruit cocktail (water-packed), ⅔ cup
Grapefruit, ½ medium
Grapes, 12
Guava, 1 medium
Honeydew, 1 2-inch wedge
Juice (unsweetened), ½ cup
Kiwi, 1 medium
Kumquats (raw), 4
Lavender gem, 1 medium
Lemon, unlimited
Loquat (raw), 10 medium
Lychees (raw), 10 medium
Mango (raw), ½ medium
Nectarine, 1 medium

Orange, 1 medium
Papaya, ½ medium
Peach, 1 medium
Persimmon, ½ medium
Pineapple (fresh, diced), ⅔ cup
Plums, 2 medium
Prunes, 2
Raisins, 2 tablespoons
Raspberries, ½ cup
Rosehips (fresh), ½ cup
Strawberries, 1 cup
Tangerine, 1 large
Watermelon, 1 cup

NOTE: We recommend that you eat whole fruit in preference to drinking fruit juices whenever possible. In that
way you gain the healthful benefits of the pectin, which
aids digestion. When you do drink fruit juices make sure
they are the natural juices with no sugar or artificial
sweeteners added. Watch your local markets and buy
local fruits in season whenever you can find them. Add
variety to your diet by trying the different melons and
fresh fruits like kiwis and pineapples that are now shipped
fresh to local supermarkets during the year.

Food Group 4: Dairy

Each serving provides 100 calories. The serving size
is noted next to each food item listed below.

Blue cheese, 1 ounce
Buttermilk, 1 cup (low-fat)
Colombo Lite Plain Yogurt, 1 cup
Cottage cheese (1% fat), ½ cup

Evaporated skim milk, ½ cup
Farmer cheese, 2 ounces
Goat's milk, ½ cup
Kefir, ½ cup
Low-fat milk (2%), ¾ cup
Nonfat dry milk (quantity needed to make 1 cup)
Other hard cheeses, 1 ounce
Other semisoft cheeses, 1 ounce
Part-skim mozzarella, 1 ounce
Part-skim ricotta, ¼ cup
Pot cheese, ¼ cup
Powdered skim milk, ⅓ cup
Skim milk, 1 cup
Swiss cheese, 1 ounce
Yogurt (plain, low-fat, active culture), ⅔ cup

NOTE: The nutrition program limits your dairy servings because even small helpings of dairy are high in calories and fat. You will find a number of varieties of low-fat cottage cheeses and yogurt on supermarket shelves, and these, along with low-fat milk and hard cheeses eaten from time to time, should be all the dairy foods you require.

Food Group 5: Protein

Each serving provides about 50 calories. A serving is usually a lean, cooked portion. The size of the portion is noted on the food list below.

Beef, 1 ounce
Chicken (white meat, no skin), 1 ounce
Clams, 5 pieces or 3 ounces

Cornish hen, 1 ounce
Crab, 2 ounces
Dried peas, beans, 1/4 cup cooked
Egg, 1
Flounder, 2 ounces
Haddock, 2 ounces
Halibut, 2 ounces
Ham, 1 ounce
Herring, 1 ounce
Lamb, 1 ounce
Liver, 1 ounce
Lobster, 2 ounces
Mackerel, 1 ounce
Mussels, 5 pieces or 3 ounces
Navy beans, 1/4 cup
Other legumes, 1/4 cup
Oysters, 5 pieces or 3 ounces
Peanut butter (natural), 2 teaspoons
Pinto beans, 1/4 cup
Pork, 1 ounce
Red beans, 1/4 cup
Salmon, 1 ounce
Sardines, 1 ounce
Scallops, 5 medium pieces
Shrimp, 5 small pieces
Sole, 2 ounces
Soybeans, 1/4 cup
Sunflower seeds, 1 tablespoon
Sprouts, 1 cup
Swordfish, 2 ounces
Tofu, 1 2-inch square
Tongue, 1 ounce
Trout, 2 ounces
Tuna (water-packed), 2 ounces

Turkey (white meat, no skin), 1 ounce
Veal, 1 ounce
Venison, 1 ounce

NOTE: Limit beef servings to four ounces (when cooked, the portion will be about the size of a woman's fist). That will use up 4 portions of your daily protein allowance. Please be aware that it takes 2 ounces of fish (as opposed to 1 ounce of meat) to provide 50 calories. So eating fish enables you to have larger servings and still stay within your daily limit. You may want to increase your intake of this food item.

Food Group 6: Healthful Desserts, Snacks, Condiments, and Beverages

Each serving provides about 100 calories. The size of each serving is noted on the food list below.

Almonds, 15
Apple butter, 3 tablespoons
Avocado, ¼ medium
Brazil nuts, 4
Butter, 1 tablespoon
Carob or cocoa powder, 4 tablespoons
Carrot juice (unsweetened), 8 ounces
Cashew nuts, 8
Decaffeinated teas, 2 to 3 cups
Filberts, 12
*Frozen yogurt, ½ cup
Frozen fruit bar, 1
Hazelnuts, 12
*Light beer, 12 ounces
*Liquor, 1 ounce

---

*Limit your intake to 2 servings per day (less is preferred).

*Mayonnaise, 1 tablespoon
Miso soup, 3 cups
Molasses (blackstrap), 4 tablespoons
Oil (olive, safflower, soy, etc.), 1 tablespoon
Oil-and-vinegar dressing, 2 tablespoons
Olives, green, 14; Greek, 4; ripe, 6
Pecans, 12 halves
Pine nuts, 12
Pistachio nuts (fresh, unsalted), 35
Popcorn (air-popped), 1 quart
Pumpkin seeds, ⅔ ounce
*Regular beer, 8 ounces
Rice cakes (large size), 3
Rice Dream Frozen Dessert, ½ cup
Sesame seeds, ⅔ ounce
Squash seeds, ⅔ ounce
Sunflower seeds, ⅔ ounce
Tomato juice (unsweetened), 16 ounces
Vegetable juice (unsweetened), 16 ounces
Walnuts, 12 halves
Water-processed decaffeinated coffee, 2 to 3 cups
Wheat germ, ¼ cup
*Wine, 3 ounces.

Miscellaneous

The following foods may be consumed in unlimited amounts and need not be counted into your plan.

Chives
Club soda
Coffee substitutes (grain beverages)
Dulse

Garlic
Ginger root
Herbal teas (nonmedicinal)
Lemon
Lime
Mustard
Oat bran
Other herbs and spices
Red chili peppers
Rice bran
Seltzer water
Tamari soy sauce (light variety), used sparingly
Vinegar
Water, bottled or tap, at least 6 to 8 8-ounce glasses daily
Wheat bran

NOTE: The snacks listed will make it possible to munch a bit between meals or to eat smaller and more frequent meals. But please heed this word of caution. Once you start eating nuts, it's hard to stop, so limit yourself and be sure that you choose unsalted nuts, raw rather than roasted.

You'll find mayonnaise on this food list. One tablespoon of mayonnaise equals one portion and you need to count mayonnaise as a portion when you use it on sandwiches or salads. Note also that herbs and spices also are included in this list and that they do not count as a food portion. Be sure to use herbs and spices to add variety and interest to recipes.

This is a sample day's menu for our 5'6" woman of small frame with a recommended weight of 125 pounds. As previously noted, her daily food list consists of the following:

Food Group 1: 6 servings
Food Group 2: 4 servings
Food Group 3: 2 servings
Food Group 4: 1 serving
Food Group 5: 5 servings
Food Group 6: 2 servings

Breakfast
V8 juice = 1 serving of Group 1 (Vegetable)
Hot or cold cereal, 1 cup = 1 serving of Group 2 (Carbo-
  hydrate)
Skim milk, ½ cup = ½ serving of Group 4 (Dairy)

Lunch
1 cup minestrone soup = 1 serving of Group 1 (Vegetable)
Tuna salad on whole-wheat toast with lettuce and tomato:
  2 servings of Group 2 (Carbohydrate) and 1 serving of Group
  5 (Protein)
  ½ serving of Group 1 (Vegetable)
Carrot and celery sticks = ½ serving of Group 1 (Vegetable)
1 apple = 1 serving of Group 3 (Fruit)

Dinner
1 baked potato topped with yogurt = 1 serving of Group 2
  (Carbohydrate) and ½ serving of Group 4 (Dairy)
4 oz. of baked chicken = 4 servings of Group 4 (Protein)
1 cup steamed broccoli = 1 serving of Group 1 (Vegetable)
Mixed salad, 2 cups = 2 servings of Group 1 (Vegetable)
2 Tbsp. salad dressing of oil and vinegar = 1 serving of Group
  6 (Desserts, Snacks, Beverages)
1 3-ounce glass of wine or Tofutti = 1 serving of Group 6
  (Desserts, Snacks, Beverages)
Bedtime snack, 1 fruit or fruit juice = 1 serving of Group 3
  (Fruit)

It's not at all difficult to plan filling yet nutritious
meals, but we'll tell you more about that in Chapter 5.
First, it's important to learn how vitamins and mineral
supplements fit into the eating plan.

UNDERSTANDING VITAMINS AND MINERALS

The Bio-Nutrionics Nutrition Plan provides you with a high-quality balanced vitamin and mineral intake. But the only one who really knows how closely you are adhering to the recommended foods and food lists is you. *If you do not get the required amount of vitamins and minerals every day in the foods you eat, you need supplements.* They are important to overall health—here's why.

Vitamins and minerals are catalysts that help the body burn fuel, build and repair cells, and produce a wide range of chemicals including essential hormones. We need an adequate supply of vitamins and minerals for these necessary bodily processes.

Interestingly, we've recently gained a great deal of knowledge about vitamins. For example, some authorities maintain that vitamin C alone will help reduce high blood cholesterol and will aid healing. It is depleted by smoking, so if you do smoke, make sure you increase your vitamin C intake. Vitamin B_1, on the other hand, has been reported to be depleted in people who drink excess alcohol. And vitamin B_6 is believed to be useful in alleviating the symptoms of premenstrual tension.

We know less about minerals. Their exact role in human nutrition is not as well defined. Dr. Richard Anderson, a researcher at the U.S. Department of Agriculture Human Research Center, says our knowledge of minerals is about twenty years behind our knowledge of vitamins. Some minerals appear in food in quantities so small that they are measured in micromilligrams. Some are recognized as essential to human health—among them potassium, calcium, magnesium, phosphorus, iron, zinc, selenium, chromium, and copper. The latter mineral is accepted today as vital to proper heart function.

Do We Really Need Vitamin and Mineral Supplements?

There is a wide range of opinion on this controversial subject. Ideally there would be no need for supplements if we were all able to get the right foods at the right time in the correct amounts. But we do not. Many of the foods we use are grown hundreds or even thousands of miles away, and foods start to lose their nutritional value from the moment they are picked. Vegetables and fruits are no longer the vitamin-rich powerhouses they were in our grandparents' day when they were picked ripe off the vine or fresh off the tree and eaten within hours. Our food today is harvested, transported, processed, frozen, and packaged before it arrives in our kitchens. There are at least thirty steps between the garden and our gullet, and at each one along the way vitamins and minerals are lost. Some experts say that as much as 50 percent or more of the nutrient value of food is lost before we eat it. Chances are, we do not get all the nutrients we need from the food we eat and most likely we need to take supplements. The question is how many should we take?

Everyone's Nutritional Needs Are Different

Although we advise supplementing your diet with vitamins and minerals we cannot, in good conscience, recommend specific dosages. Everyone's nutrient requirements differ; there simply is no such thing as a biochemically average person. You may consider yourself nutritionally "normal," but if you are a smoker, a contraceptive pill user, a person on medication or under emotional stress, or someone working in an unhealthy environment, your vitamin and mineral needs are probably very different from those of your neighbors.

In this book we offer our general recommendations for a safe and effective total daily vitamin and mineral intake (amounts that include *both* the vitamins and minerals present in the foods you eat *plus* supplements). We take the position that the government's Recommended Daily Allowances are low in many cases, particularly for vitamins E, C, and beta carotene (a vegetable form of vitamin A). These vitamins are antioxidants, and they protect the body from damage by oxidizing agents such as cigarette smoke, air pollution, and ultraviolet radiation (found in sunlight). Although our suggested allowances are higher, they are well within the safe range.

Bio-Nutrionics Recommended Daily Allowances of Vitamins and Minerals

Nutrient	*Amount*
Potassium	3,000–6,000 mg
Calcium	1,200–1,800 mg
Magnesium	600–900 mg
Phosphorus	1,000–1,600 mg
Choline	500–750 mg
Inositol	750–1,000 mg
Vitamin C	1,000–3,000 mg
Bioflavonoids	1,000–3,000 mg
Thiamin (vitamin B_1)	10–100 mg
Riboflavin (vitamin B_2)	5–50 mg
Niacin (vitamin B_3)	10–100 mg
Pantothenic acid (vitamin B_5)	50–250 mg
Pyridoxine (vitamin B_6)	10–100 mg
Vitamin B_{12}	20–200 mcg
Biotin	200–600 mcg
Folic acid	400–800 mcg
Vitamin A	5,000–15,000 IU
Beta-carotene (vegetable vitamin A)	20,000–30,000 IU

Nutrient	Amount
Vitamin D*	0–100 IU
Vitamin E	200–800 IU
Iron†	10–30 mg
Copper	4–6 mg
Zinc	20–40 mg
Manganese	10–20 mg
Chromium	100–200 mcg
Selenium	100–200 mcg
Iodine	150–300 mcg

IU = International Units

mcg = micrograms (one millionth of a gram)

mg = milligrams (one thousandth of a gram)

* Vitamin D is potentially toxic and should not be taken by most people. The exceptions are individuals who are chronically indoors, such as the elderly in nursing homes, who should perhaps receive up to 100 IU per day of vitamin D. Your doctor can do a simple blood test to see if you need a Vitamin D supplement.

†Iron supplements should not be taken indiscriminately. Those people with arthritis symptoms may have aggravation of joint problems if they take supplements containing iron. Iron supplements may be indicated by blood tests, and should then be used. Blood ferritin, measured by a blood test, generally is accepted as a good indication of your iron status. Your doctor can order this test from any clinical laboratory.

In addition to the above list of vitamins and minerals, we recommend essential fatty acids. Linseed oil is high in the Omega-3 type essential fatty acids, and is a useful supplement for many people. Take 1 teaspoon to 2 tablespoons per day of linseed oil, either directly from the bottle, or as a salad dressing (see recipe, page 140). PLEASE BE ABSOLUTELY *SURE* TO BUY FOOD-GRADE LINSEED OIL IN A FOOD STORE, AND NOT THE TYPE OF LINSEED OIL SOLD IN A HARDWARE STORE. ALSO, PLEASE REFRIGERATE THIS OIL.

This chart is to be used only as a *guide* for taking supplements. Without question, the best method is through a precise and scientific analysis of your diet and life-style. The rational way to take vitamins is first to determine your requirements, then decide how much of those requirements is provided by the foods you eat. You make up the difference with supplements. To discover the nutrient value of foods, you can check Bowes & Church's *Food Values of Portions Commonly Used* by Pennington and Church, the standard reference that's available in most libraries and bookstores. Determining your individual requirements is much more difficult; you must make specific allowances if you smoke, drink, are on medications, and so on. For this reason, we advise sophisticated evaluations. For instance, Bio-Nutrionics, Inc., in New York City has a variety of analyses that will help pinpoint your vitamin needs; many health-food stores furnish dietary questionnaires and then supply a computerized report of recommended supplements; and some software packages are available for home computers. The cost of these services is reasonable and necessary for anyone seriously interested in and concerned about his or her nutritional needs.

Tips and Hints

Although we cannot recommend specific amounts of vitamins and minerals, we can offer some valuable hints and tips:

· Space the times you take your supplements throughout the day. Some of us take them all in the morning at one time on an empty stomach. We don't eat all our foods at once and we shouldn't take our vitamins and minerals that way either. Your supplement intake should be spaced throughout the day, and with your meals so the vitamins and minerals are digested and used in exactly the same way as those in the food you eat.

· Iron and vitamin C always should be taken together.

· Iron and vitamin E should always be taken separately.

· If you have trouble sleeping, try taking your calcium and magnesium supplements at bedtime.

· If you've never used supplements, begin taking them gradually, increasing your dosage over time.

· If you experience any reactions to supplements, such as diarrhea and nausea, you may be sensitive to one or more ingredients in the supplement. Switch to another brand and seek out hypoallergenic supplements.

THERE'S NOTHING BETTER THAN A HEALTHY DIET

As we mentioned before, while vitamins and minerals are extremely important to good health, they cannot take the place of a balanced diet. That is what the food plan is all about. It is the heart of Bio-Nutrionics and you will refer to this chapter again and again over the next thirty days. Eventually you'll learn the food lists and their values by heart.

In the next chapter you will learn there is nothing confining about this diet. You can eat out as often as you like, wherever you please. We will offer some helpful tips to guide you. On the other hand, if cooking is your specialty, there are delicious recipes that provide variety and complete, balanced nutrition. The best recommendation for the Bio-Nutrionics Program are the people who are on it . . . people who have lost weight, regained energy, and lowered their cholesterol. You can do it too!

5. Putting the Nutrition Plan to Work

This chapter will guide you in planning meals, offer shopping and cooking tips, and suggest recommendations for ordering food when dining out.

The appeal of the Bio-Nutrionics food lists is in their variety of tasty and filling foods, so it's not difficult to put the plan to work. Be open to new flavors and textures as you read the pages that follow, such as the nutty crunch of Almond Crunch Granola or the tanginess of Carrots Raspberry, a side dish that's almost addictive. The seventy-one easy-to-follow recipes included here will offer some unique variations on favorite dishes (like griddle cakes or chili) as well as new treats. We are even going to give you a supermarket shopping list to start you out on the right foot.

First, some interesting hints and tips:

TIP SHEET

Here is a variety of valuable tips. Some will save you time and money; others will help you understand the foods allowed on the Nutrition Plan and offer interesting ways to include them in your daily diet.

On Stock

Many recipes call for stock of one kind or another, either chicken, fish, meat, or vegetable. We recommend the homemade variety, which is easy and inexpensive to make (see directions below). To make a strong homemade stock, save the broth from chicken or fish that has been poached and store the broth in separate containers in the freezer. When you're ready to make chicken or fish stock, add the stored containers to the recipe. If you own a Crock-Pot you can begin your stock in the evening and let it cook overnight. Otherwise use any large pot. If you use canned stock, make sure it's low-sodium.

Chicken Stock: Place inexpensive pieces of chicken, such as the neck, back, and wings, or the carcass of a roasted chicken, or both, in a large pot or Crock-Pot. Cover the pieces of chicken with water and any reserved chicken broth you may have in your freezer. Add to this a couple of stalks of celery, including the tops; a cut-up, cleaned not peeled carrot; a bay leaf; and a peeled medium onion, cut in half. If you have small packets of mixed herbs, toss 'em in. Add about ten whole peppercorns. Bring to a boil and let simmer for at least an hour. Taste for flavor. Add salt substitute if necessary. Drain. Store and freeze for later use. Before serving, skim fat off top.

Fish Stock: Proceed as you would for chicken stock, replacing the chicken parts with fish heads and bones. (The exception to this rule is lobster heads. Do not use them in the preparation of a seafood stock.) To increase the strength of the stock, you can add a bottle of clam juice, but be careful of its sodium content. If you are on a low-sodium diet, omit clam juice.

Meat Stock: Ask your butcher for two to three pounds

of beef and veal bones. You may have to pay for them, but the cost will be slight. Place bones in a moderate oven, at about 350°, and let the bones roast until nicely brown. Remove and discard the fat that accumulates in the pan. Put the bones in the Crock-Pot or large pot and proceed exactly as you would for chicken stock.

On Fish

The rule to follow for cooking fish is 10 minutes per inch of thickness. For example, if the fish is only a half-inch thick, it will require 5 to 6 minutes to cook, regardless of whether you are broiling, baking, or sauté-ing it.

Try new varieties of fish. There's an oceanful to draw from, and you may be surprised how you'll come to love the different delicate flavors.

According to a study by the U.S. Department of Agriculture, the fat content of different types of fish varies considerably. Get to know the fatty fishes from the lean as it will help guide you in preparation. Lean fish has less than 2 percent fat. Cod is a good lean fish, as are others in the cod family: haddock, scrod, whiting, and pollack; all these along with mackerel, which is in the moderate-fat category (between 2 percent and 6 percent), are all rich in Omega-3 oils. You'll find the leaner fish excellent for sauces and salad. Other species of fish like bass, pike, sole, halibut, perch, snapper, and rockfish are also lean.

In the fatty group (over 6 percent fat are salmon, swordfish, fresh tuna, bluefish, and, as you may have guessed, butterfish. The fattier fish contains enough natural oil of its own and therefore requires little or no oil when cooking. This group is not to be avoided because of its higher fat content. In fact, try to eat the following varieties more often, since they are an even greater source of Omega-3 oil: herring, mackerel, halibut, salmon, rainbow trout, and sardines.

And who among us can exist without canned tuna, salmon, and sardines. We've come to depend on them over the years. But we ask that you buy tuna packed in water. Sardines usually come packed in oil, sometimes olive oil, but either way they do tend to have a high sodium content. To be safe, drain the can before using them. Sardines are extremely healthy; we've heard them called a "tonic for the heart."

On Labels

We cannot stress enough the importance of reading labels on the foods you buy. Labels contain information vital to your health. Not only will you find the calories per portion listed on most items today, but you will also find the sodium content. Many packaged goods also list amounts of fats, carbohydrates, potassium, and protein. And given the urgency of "cholesterol overload," we predict they will soon carry the cholesterol contents as well. Ingredients are listed in descending order of proportion. For example, the product contains the most of the first ingredient listed and the least of the last, with the ingredients in between in their respective proportions. Whenever possible buy low-sodium products, especially when our recipes call for them.

On Salads

What do you think of when you hear the word *salad*? A bunch of green things on a plate, dripping with dressing? Now's the time to use your imagination, to get creative! We've listed below some items to mix into your assorted greens to make your salad a melody of color and texture:

Kidney beans	Cannellini beans
Chick-peas	Chinese pea pods
Mushrooms	Beets
Walnuts, broken up	Artichoke hearts
Sunflower seeds	Scallions
Carrots	Hard-boiled egg whites
Broccoli florets	Fresh peas
Whole-wheat croutons	Bits of flaked tuna

These are but a few suggestions. Make your own additions using the food lists as a guide.

MENU PLANNING

Here is a week of sample meals as a guide to your menu planning.

Please understand that these are only suggestions. You have a whole universe of foods to choose from in the food lists in Chapter 4. For example, if you dislike tuna fish, find a substitute among the many selections offered. If hot cereal doesn't appeal to you or you don't have the time to prepare it, try our low-fat, low-calorie, High-Energy Drink instead. It's breakfast for winners that takes seconds to prepare.

But be alert to the importance of a hot breakfast, especially oatmeal, which actually lowers cholesterol. Try to have it several times a week.

Starred foods can be found in the recipe section of the book.

The best thirst quencher in the world is water. After that, hot herbal tea is the recommended drink.

Breakfast

Day 1   tomato or V8 juice
oatmeal with skim milk
Whole-Wheat Bread,* toast with honey

Day 2   ½ a grapefruit
whole-grain cereal with skim milk
½ a whole-wheat English muffin with Fruit Jam*

Day 3   apple juice
Cream of Rice (preferably brown)
toasted Five-Grain Bread* with Fruit Jam*

Day 4   1 slice of whole-wheat toast
High-Energy Breakfast Drink*

Day 5   juice or ½ grapefruit
yogurt with banana
Cranberry Muffin*

Day 6   melon sections
Griddle Cakes* with Strawberry Sauce*

Day 7   juice
Almond Crunch Granola* with skim milk
Bran Muffin*

Lunch

Day 1   Chicken Salad* on Five-Grain Bread*
garnish with lettuce and tomato
fresh fruit cocktail

Day 2   tuna salad on whole-wheat bread
carrot sticks

Day 3   Quick Chili*
green salad
corn muffin

Day 4   Tuna and Cannellini Salad*
whole-wheat toast
apple

Day 5   pasta salad
           Cranberry Muffin*
           fruit salad

Day 6   chef's salad with 30-Day Salad Dressing*
           Five-Grain Bread*

Day   Bean and Spinach Soup*
           green salad (see salad tips)
           Gelatin*

Dinner

Day 1   Fish Fillets with Mustard Sauce*
           brown rice
           Carrots Raspberry*
           Apple Raisin Crisp*

Day 2   Pennsylvania Dutch Vegetable Soup*
           green salad (see salad tips)
           Crème de Cream*

Day 3   Risotto alla Milanese* with chicken added
           green salad (see salad tips)
           fruit

Day 4   Carrot Curry Soup*
           Tofu Burger* on whole-wheat English muffin
           garnish with lettuce, tomato, and onion
           Banana/Strawberry "Ice Cream"*

Day 5   Stir-Fry Beef and Vegetables*
           brown rice
           Sugar-free Gelatin*

Day 6   Pasta Gretchen*
           Zucchini Italian Style*
           fresh fruit salad

Day 7   Chicken in Cream Sauce*
           broccoli with lemon
           Paul's Potatoes*
           Corn Shortcake*

STOCKING UP

Before beginning your new life plan to lowering cholesterol, check your larder against this list. Then stock up on some of these suggested products.

Breakfast Cereals
  Hot
    Oatmeal (best choice)
    Mother's Oat Bran
    Wheatena
    Cream of Wheat (preferably whole wheat)
    Cream of Rice (preferably brown rice)
  Cold
    Granola, unsweetened
    Nutri-Grain
    Shredded Wheat
    Puffed wheat, corn, or rice

Breads and Crackers
    Whole-wheat pita bread
    Whole grain breads (available at health-food stores)
    Whole-wheat English muffins
    Finn Crisps
    Rice cakes
    Wasa Lite Rye
    Ideal Flatbread
    100% whole-wheat matzo

Beans, Rice, and Grains
    Any fresh or dried beans, peas and lentils (Pinto, kidney, navy, and white (cannellini) are among those suggested)
    Brown rice, long- and short-grain
    Whole-wheat flour
    Wheat germ
    Unprocessed bran
    Buckwheat groats (kasha)
    Corn chips
    Corn or flour tortillas

Pasta: whole-wheat, spinach, artichoke, or pasta made with semolina, if others are not available

Fish, canned
    Tuna, packed in water
    Sardines, packed in water or olive oil
    Mackerel
    Salmon

Sauces and Salad Dressings
    Prego No-salt Spaghetti Sauce
    Ronzoni Lite Natural Marinara Sauce
    Paul Newman's Marinara Sauce
    Aunt Millie's Marinara Sauce
    Dijon-style mustards
    Vinegars, red and white wine, balsamic, cider, raspberry, etc.
    Paul Newman's Italian Dressing
    Hain's natural French, eggless Mayo
    Old El Paso, Ortega, or Tio Sancho Taco, Salsa and Hot Sauces
    Linseed oil (Hain's—obtainable at health-food stores)
    Olive oil
    Safflower oil
    Walnut oil
    Sesame oil
    Tamari Lite Soy Sauce
    Herbs, assorted dried (look for packets that can be immersed in soups)

Soups
    Various bean, pea, and legume types with first choice given to those types with a vegetarian, nonmeat base. Also suggested is minestrone, vegetable, tomato, Manhattan clam chowder, mushroom barley, low-sodium chicken broth, or onion soup: Progresso, Health Valley, and Campbell's are brands to look for. Always check the label to see if the product is low in sodium.

Miscellaneous
    Salt substitutes (Vegit, Season-Al, or Mrs. Dash)
    Dried fruits

Walnuts
Raisins
Sunflower seeds, unsalted
In the "Fridge"
Yogurt, plain low-fat
Milk, skim
Farmer cheese
Cottage cheese, low-fat
Ricotta, low-fat
Mozzarella, part-skim
Fruit, assorted in season
Salad greens
Salad accompaniments (see tips on salads)

RECIPE INDEX

Breakfast
Almond Crunch Granola
Griddle Cakes
High-Energy Breakfast Drink
Oatmeal Pancakes

Soups
Pennsylvania Dutch Vegetable Soup
Bean and Spinach Soup
Cream of Broccoli Soup
Carrot Curry Soup
Leek and Potato Soup
Gertrude's Vegetable and Bean Soup
Fish Chowder

Main Dishes
Tofu Burger
Quick Chili
Fish Fillets with Mustard Sauce
Stir-Fry Beef and Vegetables
Spiced Chicken Salad
Chicken in Cream Sauce
Salmon Loaf

Sautéed Tofu with Broccoli and Cashews
Tuna Jambalaya
Marinated Flounder, Chinese Style
Baked Whole Fish
Poached Salmon
Chicken Dinner in a Pot
Tuna and Cannellini Salad

Rice, Pasta, Grains, and Bread
Bulgur with Garlic (Cracked Wheat)
Five-Grain Bread
Sesame Pasta Salad
Whole-Wheat Bread
Fiesta Pasta Picnic Salad
Risotto alla Milanese (Italian Rice)
Polenta, Plain and Fancy
Pasta Gretchen
Pasta and Clam Sauce
Lentil Salad
Hummus (Bean Dip)
Shirley's Bran Muffins
Pumpkin Nut Muffins
Blueberry Muffins
Cranberry Bread
Golden Sauerkraut and Noodles

Vegetables
Warm Beet Salad
Escarole, Braised with Garlic
Baked Zucchini
Zucchini and Tomato Italian Style
Carrots Raspberry
Spicy Wok Broccoli
Braised Celery
Paul's Potatoes
Autumn Casserole

Sauces and Salad Dressings
Strawberry Sauce
Tomato Sauce
Mayonnaise

Dijon Salad Dressing
Linseed Oil Dressing
Black Bean Sauce
Sweet-and-Sour Sauce
Oriental Marinade

Desserts
Sugar-free Gelatin
Indian Pudding
Apple Raisin Crisp
Banana/Strawberry "Ice Cream"
Accidental Mousse
Mustard Gingerbread
Crême de Cream
Tofu Whipped Cream
Mary Theresa's Corn Shortbread
Velvet Pumpkin Cream Pie
Flaky Pie Crust

Miscellaneous
Green Drink
Fruit Jam

Important Note

A breakdown of the number of portions of each of the six food groups is included for each recipe.

BREAKFAST

Almond Crunch Granola

2 Tbsp. sesame oil
¼ cup maple syrup or honey
6 cups rolled oats
¼ cup chopped almonds

Mix the oil and honey or maple syrup together. (Cinnamon and vanilla extract can be added in the oil-honey mixture for taste, if desired.) Stir in oats and almonds. Bake on a cookie sheet at 300° until golden and crisp. Let cool and store in a jar in a dark, cool place.
Serves 12.

Each serving is made up of: 1 Grain portion
1¼ Healthful Dessert portions

Griddle Cakes

½ cup whole-wheat flour
⅛ cup wheat germ
⅛ cup unprocessed bran
½ cup skim milk
1 egg white
⅛ tsp. tamari
oil to coat pan

Place all ingredients in food processor or blender and blend thoroughly. Coat griddle pan with oil. Drop batter by tablespoons onto pan, turning once. Serve with Strawberry Sauce.
Makes 10 griddle cakes.

Each 3-griddle-cake serving is made up of: 1 Grain portion

High-Energy Breakfast Drink

8 oz. skim milk
1 small banana, or 1 small apple, cored with skin left on
1 Tbsp. wheat germ
1 Tbsp. unprocessed bran
vanilla, dash

Place all the ingredients in a blender or food processor
and blend well.
Serves 1.

Each serving is made up of: with banana 2½ Fruit portions
1 Dairy portion
with apple 2 Fruit portions
1 Dairy portion

Oatmeal Pancakes

1½ cups regular rolled oats, *not* instant
1½ cups skim milk
½ cup whole-wheat flour
1 tsp. baking powder
½ tsp. ground cinnamon
1 Tbsp. safflower oil
1 tsp. honey
2 egg whites, beaten

Place oats and milk in blender and let stand 1 minute.
Add flour, baking powder, and cinnamon. Blend. Add safflower oil, honey, and egg whites, and blend again, scraping
down sides if necessary. Heat griddle pan until a drop of water
spatters.
Pour batter onto griddle, enough to make a 3-inch griddle
cake, about ⅛ cup. Cook each cake until puffed, turn, brown
other side.
Yields 16 cakes.

Each 3-cake serving is made up of: 2 Grain portions

SOUPS

Pennsylvania Dutch Vegetable Soup

6 cups water
1 lb. lean beef, from flank or foreshank
2 sliced onions
2 stalks celery, cut in one-inch slices
4 pared beets, sliced to equal 2 cups
4 carrots, sliced thin
1 small cabbage, cut in wedges
1 bay leaf
1 cup beets, grated
2 tsp. salt substitute
1 6-oz. can tomato sauce, low-sodium
1 Tbsp. honey
2 Tbsp. white vinegar
½ pint low-fat yogurt

Place water, beef, onion, celery, *sliced* beets, carrots, cabbage, bay leaf, and salt substitute in large stockpot. Cover and simmer about 2 hours. Add grated beets, tomato paste, honey, and vinegar. Simmer 15 minutes more.

Up to this point the soup can be made the day before. Cool and refrigerate.

To serve, skim off fat and bring to a boil over medium heat. Lower heat and simmer, covered, for 10 minutes. Top with a dollop of yogurt before serving.

This soup freezes well.

Serves 8.

Each serving is made up of: 1 Protein portion
                            3 Vegetable portions

Bean and Spinach Soup

1 cup dried white beans
2 qts. boiling water
1 bay leaf
1 medium onion, chopped
1 clove garlic, chopped
2 Tbsp. olive oil
2 cups water
2 low-sodium beef bouillon cubes
1 16-oz. package frozen chopped spinach, or 1 lb. fresh
  spinach, if available
1 Tbsp. flour blended with 2 Tbsp. cold water
freshly ground pepper

Cover beans with 2 quarts boiling water. Add bay leaf.
Cover pot and let stand for 1 hour. Sauté onion and garlic in
2 tablespoons of oil until transparent. Add to bean pot and
simmer until the beans are soft, about 2 hours.

Add the water, bouillon, and spinach. Bring to boil and
stir in the flour-and-water mixture slowly. Grind in fresh pepper to taste. Taste for flavor. If necessary add salt substitute.
Serves 4.

Each serving is made up of: 1 Grain portion
                           1 Vegetable portion

Cream of Broccoli Soup

2 cups broccoli (1 small head), cut up
1 Tbsp. olive oil
1 medium onion
½ tsp. dry mustard
1 cup skim milk
2 Tbsp. whole-wheat flour
1 cup homemade chicken or vegetable broth, or 1 10-
  oz. can low-sodium
½ Tbsp. ground coriander
freshly ground pepper
dash of low-sodium soy sauce
½ cup low-fat yogurt

Steam broccoli until tender and purée in food processor or blender. Use stalk as well as florets. Coat a 1-quart saucepan with olive oil and over medium heat; sauté onion until transparent. Stir in mustard.

Place flour and milk in a tightly covered jar and shake until well blended. Add to onions in pan and cook until thickened. Add puréed broccoli, coriander, pepper, and soy sauce. Cook over low heat until heated through and well blended. May be cooked ahead to this point and refrigerated.

Blend yogurt with a bit of the soup in a small container, add to soup, and heat just before serving.

Serves 4.

Each serving is made up of: ¾ Dairy portion
1 Vegetable portion

Carrot Curry Soup

2 Tbsp. oil, preferably olive
2 medium onions, chopped
1½ Tbsp. curry powder
2 lbs. carrots, peeled and sliced
dash of tamari or low-sodium soy sauce
¼ cup chopped fresh coriander or 1 Tbsp. dried
1½ quarts chicken stock, preferably homemade or low-sodium
2 cups plain yogurt (if soup is to be served cold)
1½ cups skim milk (if soup is to be served hot)
scallions or parsley for garnish

Heat oil in saucepan and cook onions until transparent. Blend in curry powder and sauté for about 3 minutes. Add carrots, tamari or soy sauce, coriander, and stock. Bring to a boil and simmer for 20 minutes. Turn soup into food processor or blender and purée. You may have to do this 2 cups at a time to avoid overloading.

If soup is to be served hot, return to pan, add milk, and heat.
For cold soup, refrigerate after puréeing. Blend in yogurt

before serving. Garnish with thinly sliced scallions or chopped parsley.
Serves 8.

Each serving is made up of: 1 Dairy portion
1 Vegetable portion

Leek and Potato Soup

2 Tbsp. olive oil
1 bunch of leeks, sliced, using some of the green tops, to make about 4 cups
2 cloves of garlic, mashed or chopped
2 medium potatoes, peeled and cut in chunks
4 cups strong chicken stock (see Tips) or use low-sodium canned
dash salt (optional)
white pepper to taste
1 cup skim milk

In large pot, sauté leeks and garlic in oil. Stir until leeks are just limp. Add potatoes and stock and bring to a boil. Lower heat and simmer 20 minutes, or until leeks and potatoes are tender. Purée in food processor or blender 2 cups at a time to avoid overloading. Season with salt and pepper. Return to pot and add milk and reheat. Leftover soup may be frozen.
Serves 8.

Each serving is made up of: ½ Grain portion
½ Dairy portion
1 Vegetable portion

Gertrude's Vegetable and Bean Soup

2 Tbsp. olive oil
1¼ cup onions, chopped
1 clove garlic, crushed
7 cups water*
3 cups tomatoes, diced
2 tsp. paprika
½ tsp. light tamari, or light soy sauce
1½ tsp. thyme leaves, crushed, or 1 tsp. dried
¾ tsp. sage leaves, crushed
freshly ground pepper to taste
¼ cup barley
1 cup lentils
1 cup green beans, sliced
1 cup carrots, sliced
1 cup celery, sliced
¼ cup parsley, chopped
½ cup scallions, sliced for garnish (optional)

Heat oil in large stockpot. Add onions and garlic. Sauté about 5 minutes. Add water, tomatoes, paprika, tamari or soy sauce, thyme, sage, and pepper. Bring to boil. Add barley. Reduce heat and simmer covered until barley is partially cooked, about 40 minutes. Add lentils and simmer covered for 10 minutes more. Add green beans, carrots, celery, and parsley, then simmer until vegetables are just tender, about 12 minutes. Leftovers may be frozen.

Serves 10.

*You can replace water with vegetable stock; add appropriate food values.

Each serving is made up of: ½ Grain portion
1 Vegetable portion

Fish Chowder

1 onion, chopped
2 cups mushrooms, coarsely chopped
1 Tbsp. olive oil
Vegit
2 celery stalks, chopped
1 cup rolled oats
white pepper, to taste
thyme, dash
basil, dash
1 bay leaf
1 lb. white fish, such as cod
6 cups water
1 6″ strip kombu seaweed, also known as kelp (optional)

Sauté onion, celery, and mushrooms in oil. Add sprinkling of Vegit. Add oats, water, kombu, and herbs. Cook 15 minutes. Remove seaweed, chop, and return to pan. Remove bay leaf. Blend half the soup in blender for creamy texture. Add fish and cook 10 minutes. Season with Vegit.
Serves 8.

Each serving is made up of: ½ Grain portion
1 Protein portion
1 Vegetable portion

MAIN DISHES

Tofu Burger

30 oz. tofu
6 Tbsp. grated carrots
4 Tbsp. chopped scallions
2 Tbsp. sesame seeds
½ cup whole-wheat flour
2 Tbsp. tamari
3 Tbsp. peanut oil for sautéeing

Mash tofu with a fork until crumbled. Combine tofu, grated carrots, chopped scallions, sesame seed, flour, and tamari. Knead all ingredients well as if kneading bread. Shape dough into 8 patties. Heat oil in skillet. Sauté patties in hot oil until both sides are golden brown. Drain on absorbent paper. Serve on whole-wheat bread or whole-wheat rolls.

Tofu Burgers may also be broiled, after first brushing with oil.

Garnish with mustard, tomato, ketchup, lettuce, pickles, onion rings.

Serves 8.

Each serving is made up of: ¼ Healthful Dessert portion
2 Protein portions

Quick Chili

2 15-oz. cans of red kidney beans, drained
1 1-lb. can of stewed tomatoes, low-sodium, if available
1½ Tbsp. chili powder
6 shakes of Tabasco sauce
1 Tbsp. garlic, minced
1 Tbsp. cumin
2 shakes salt substitute
2 oz. port or red wine
1 medium onion, chopped

Place all ingredients in saucepan and stir together. Heat until all flavors are blended and hot.

Serves 2 as a main dish; 4 as a side dish.

Each serving is made up of: 5 Grain portions
1 Vegetable portion

Variations: To make this dish into Chili con Carne, add ¼ lb. of lean chopped meat sautéed in one tablespoon of olive oil.

For a cool creamy flavor, top with a dollop of yogurt.

Fish Fillets with Mustard Sauce

3 Tbsp. Dijon mustard
2 Tbsp. cider vinegar
1 tsp. honey
4 Tbsp. olive oil
1 Tbsp. chopped fresh dill
1 Tbsp. low-fat yogurt
1 lb. fish fillets. Use any firm-fleshed white fish, such as
    scrod, flounder, sole, monk, or cod

In a small bowl combine mustard, vinegar, and honey.
With wire whisk add oil a tablespoon at a time. Mixture should
be thick. Fold in dill and yogurt. Let marinate for at least half
an hour.

Wash fish off and pat dry with paper towels. Coat pan
lightly with oil. Coat fish heavily with the marinade. Bake in
preheated 350° oven until fish flakes easily, about 10 minutes.
Place under broiler to brown top.

This dish may be broiled instead of baked. Place pan about
4 inches from broiling unit so as not to burn.

Tip: Save any leftover marinade to use as a salad dressing.
Add more yogurt to thin.

Serves 3.

Each serving is made up of: 1 Healthful Dessert portion
                          3½ Protein portions

Stir-Fry Beef and Vegetables

¾ lb. lean boneless round beef
2 tsp. olive oil
2 tsp. sesame oil
⅓ cup carrots, sliced on the diagonal
⅓ cup onions, sliced
⅓ cup celery, sliced on the diagonal
5 to 6 mushrooms, cut in quarters
3 oz. Chinese pea pods, fresh or frozen (½ of 6-oz. package)
2 cups fresh bean sprouts
½ Tbsp. cornstarch
½ tsp. ground ginger
1 clove garlic, mashed
1 Tbsp. soy or tamari sauce
¼ cup sherry

Trim fat from beef and slice into thin strips. Heat olive oil in wok and add beef over moderately high heat, turning until meat is no longer red. Remove and reserve. Add sesame oil to pan and heat. Add carrots and stir-fry 1 or 2 minutes. Add onion, celery, mushrooms, pea pods, and bean sprouts, and continue to stir-fry until vegetables are tender but still crisp, about 3 to 4 minutes.

Mix cornstarch, ginger, and garlic with soy sauce and sherry in small container until smooth and slowly add to vegetables, stirring constantly. Return beef to wok, reduce heat, cover pan for a minute for flavors to blend.

Serves 4.

Each serving is made up of: (beef) 1 Healthful Dessert
portion
3 Protein portions
1 Vegetable portion
(chicken) ½ Healthful Dessert
portion
3 Protein portions
1 Vegetable portion

Spiced Chicken Salad

1 cup cooked brown rice
¼ cup low-fat yogurt
1 Tbsp. honey
1 tsp. grated lemon peel
¼ tsp. ground ginger
1½ cups cooked chicken*, cubed
¾ cup grapes, cut in half
¼ cup almonds, slivered, unsalted

Cook rice (⅓ cup of raw rice to ⅔ cup of water will make 1 cup of cooked rice). Combine yogurt, honey, lemon peel, and ginger. Stir in into rice, fold in chicken, and top with grapes and almonds.
Serves 4.
*Use previously baked or poached chicken.

Each serving is made up of: ½ Grain portion
1 Healthful Dessert portion
3 Protein portions

Chicken in Cream Sauce

2 Tbsp. olive oil
½ tsp. garlic, minced
2 boneless chicken breasts, skinned and cut in half to
  make four pieces
1 Tbsp. flour, whole-wheat if possible
½ cup skim milk
½ cup chicken broth, low-sodium
herb seasoning mixture
juice of half a lemon

Heat oil in skillet and add garlic and chicken. Cover pan and let cook for 15 or 20 minutes until tender and brown. (Cooking time depends on the size of the chicken breasts.) Remove to heated platter to keep warm.
While the chicken is cooking, place the flour and milk in

a jar with a tight lid and shake well. Add it to the skillet after the chicken is removed and stir with a wire whisk. This will get quite thick. Quickly add the broth and continue to stir. Add seasoning and lemon juice. Stir again and return the chicken to the skillet, cover pan, and heat through for a couple of minutes so the flavors can blend.
Serves 4.

Each serving is made up of: 1 Healthful Dessert portion
3 Protein portions

Salmon Loaf

1 onion, large, chopped
1 stalk celery, chopped
Vegit, to taste
1 7-oz. can salmon
2 cups bulgur, cooked
½ tsp. thyme
¼ tsp. white pepper
¼ cup ketchup (honey-sweetened type)
¼ cup parsley, chopped
1 clove garlic, chopped
1 egg white, whipped
sesame oil, a few drops

Preheat oven to 350°.
Sauté onion and celery in a few drops of sesame oil. Season with Vegit. Combine with salmon, bulgur, thyme, pepper, ketchup, parsley, and garlic. Fold in egg white. Place in oiled baking dish and bake 20 minutes.
Serves 4.

Each serving is made up of: 1 Grain portion
2 Protein portions
½ Vegetable portion

Sautéed Tofu with Broccoli and Cashews

2 Tbsp. sesame oil
1 medium onion, chopped
½ cup cashew nuts
1 bunch of broccoli florets
1 lb. tofu, cubed
2 Tbsp. tamari or light soy sauce

Heat skillet, add oil. When hot, add chopped onion and cashews. When onions become translucent, add broccoli and simmer for 2 minutes. Add tofu and tamari. Simmer 5 minutes.
Serves 6.

Each serving is made up of: ½ Healthful Dessert portion
1 Protein portion
1 Vegetable portion

Tuna Jambalaya

1½ cups celery, chopped
¾ cup onion, chopped
½ green pepper, chopped
2 cloves garlic, chopped
1 Tbsp. olive oil
2 cups chicken stock, homemade or low-sodium (may also use vegetable stock)
1 cup brown rice, raw
1 28-oz. can tomatoes, low-sodium
1 bay leaf
3 drops Tabasco
½ tsp. red pepper, crushed
¼ tsp. thyme
2 6½-oz. cans water-packed tuna, low-sodium
¼ cup fresh parsley, chopped

In skillet, cook celery, onion, green pepper, and garlic in olive oil for 5 minutes. Add stock, rice, tomatoes, bay leaf,

Tabasco, red pepper, and thyme. Simmer, covered, for 30 minutes, or until rice is done. Drain tuna and break up. Add tuna and parsley to cooked rice mixture and heat through.
Serves 6.

Each serving is made up of: ½ Grain portion
2 Protein portions
2 Vegetable portions

Marinated Flounder, Chinese Style

4 Tbsp. light soy sauce
1 Tbsp. sesame oil
1 tsp. ground ginger
¼ tsp. garlic, chopped
½ tsp. honey
1 tsp. balsamic vinegar
2 Tbsp. water, or a combination of sherry and water
1½ lbs. of filleted flounder, or any white firm-fleshed fish

Mix soy sauce, oil, ginger, garlic, honey, vinegar and water or water and sherry combined in a jar and shake well. Pour contents over fish and marinate for 15 minutes. Drain and reserve sauce. Transfer fish to broiling pan and broil, basting with the reserved sauce. Remember the rule for cooking fish: 10 minutes for every inch of thickness.
Serves 4.
Note: Because this marinade is used as a basting sauce, most of the sodium is not retained.

Each serving is made up of: 3 Protein portions

Baked Whole Fish

A quick and tasty way to prepare a fresh-caught trout, mackerel, or other small white fish.

>   4 fresh lake trout, or other small white fish (about 4 oz.
>   after cleaning)
>   2 Tbsp. olive oil
>   1/2 cup parsley, chopped
>   1/2 cup fresh dill, chopped, or 1 Tbsp. dried
>   1/4 cup fresh chives, chopped, or 2 Tbsp. dried
>   1/4 cup onions, chopped
>   2 Tbsp. fresh lemon juice
>   lemon slices (optional)

Preheat oven to 400°.
Clean and rinse fish. Pat dry. In a small bowl mix together the oil, parsley, dill, chives, onion, and lemon juice. Divide mixture into four parts and stuff each fish. Wrap each fish individually in aluminum foil, sealing the edges carefully. Bake 20 minutes. May be garnished with lemon slices.
Serves 4.

Each serving is made up of: 1 1/4 Healthful Dessert portion
4 Protein portions

Poached Salmon

>   1 lb. salmon fillet
>   1 6" strip kombu (seaweed; optional)
>   1/2 cup rolled oats
>   2 Tbsp. fresh lemon juice
>   1/8 tsp. soy sauce
>   1 large onion, diced
>   2 cups water
>   1 Tbsp. sesame tahini

In a skillet place the salmon and partially cover with water, about halfway. Bring to just boiling and then simmer about 10 minutes. The fish is done when it turns pink. Remember the rule for cooking fish: 10 minutes for every inch of thickness. Remove fish and place on warm serving dish.

To prepare the sauce, place the kombu, if using, the oats, 2 Tbsp. lemon juice, soy sauce, onion, water, and tahini in a saucepan, and cook on medium heat for 15 minutes. Remove seaweed. Pour contents into blender and blend until smooth. Pour over salmon.

Serves 4.

Each serving is made up of: 1¼ Healthful Dessert portions
4 Protein portions
¼ Vegetable portion

Chicken Dinner in a Pot

2 chicken breasts, split and skinned
4 medium potatoes, peeled and thickly sliced
2 large carrots, peeled and quartered
½ lb. fresh green beans, or 1 10-oz. package frozen
1 large onion, sliced
1 Tbsp. dried parsley flakes
Vegit, to taste
freshly ground pepper
½ cup beef stock, homemade or low-sodium

Preheat oven to 300°.

Place chicken breasts in a large, heavy ovenware casserole. Place sliced potatoes on top of chicken. Cut quartered carrots into 2-inch lengths. Cut off ends of beans, or separate frozen beans, and place in pot with the onions and carrots. Sprinkle with parsley flakes and season lightly with Vegit and pepper. Pour stock over all and cover tightly. Bake 2 hours or until vegetables are tender.

Serves 4.

Each serving is made up of: 1 Grain portion
3 Protein portions
1 Vegetable portion

Tuna and Cannellini Salad

2 20-oz. cans of white cannellini beans
2 7-oz. cans of albacore tuna, packed in water
1/2 cup chopped onions
1/4 cup chopped parsley
1 small carrot, chopped
2 Tbsp. olive oil
4 Tbsp. fresh lemon juice
freshly ground pepper, to taste

Rinse beans thoroughly in cold water and drain. Pat dry. Drain tuna and flake. Chop onions, parsley, and carrot in food processor. Combine with tuna and beans. Add oil, lemon juice, and pepper and toss gently.
Serves 6.

Each serving is made up of: 2 Grain portions
3/4 Healthful Dessert portion
1 Protein portion
1/4 Vegetable portion

RICE, PASTA, GRAINS, AND BREAD

Bulgur with Garlic

A staple of the Middle-Eastern diet, bulgur is really cracked wheat. It's wonderfully easy to prepare and a perfect side dish in place of potatoes, rice, or pasta. So healthy!

1/2 cup bulgur
1 Tbsp. olive oil
1 cup homemade or low-sodium canned chicken stock
1 clove garlic, chopped
1 Tbsp. parsley, chopped

In a skillet, sauté the bulgur in oil for about 2 minutes, until the bulgur is coated and the grains separate. Add stock

and cook until the bulgur is tender and the liquid absorbed—
about 10 minutes. Stir in the garlic and parsley, and cook
another minute or two.

Serves 2 (double recipe for 4).

Each serving is made up of: 2 Grain portions
$\frac{1}{2}$ Healthful Dessert portion

Five-Grain Bread

1½ cups boiling water
¾ cup cracked wheat (bulgur)
1 cup buttermilk
¼ cup molasses
2 Tbsp. honey
4 Tbsp. safflower oil
1 tsp. light tamari
2 envelopes dry yeast
¼ cup very warm water
2 cups white flour
½ cup bran
½ cup wheat flakes
2 cups whole-wheat flour
1 egg, beaten
1 Tbsp. poppy seeds

Pour boiling water over cracked wheat. Let stand for 1
hour. Heat together the buttermilk, molasses, honey, oil, and
tamari. Stir and cool to lukewarm. Sprinkle yeast over ¼ cup
warm water. Let proof for 10 minutes. Add to buttermilk
mixture along with white flour and beat for 2 minutes until
smooth. Stir in cracked wheat, bran, and wheat flakes. Slowly
add whole-wheat flour, stirring until a nice firm dough is
formed. Turn onto floured surface and knead 10 minutes
until elastic and shiny. Add more white flour if necessary to
keep from sticking. Place in large oiled bowl and let rise in
warm place until doubled in volume. Punch down, knead on
floured surface a few times, then let rest for 10 minutes. Divide
and shape into two loaves. Place in greased pans, cover, and

let rise again until doubled. Brush top with beaten egg and sprinkle with poppy seeds. Bake at 350° for 45 minutes until well browned.
    Yields 2 loaves, 20 slices per loaf.

Each serving is made up of: 1 Grain portion
                           ½ Healthful Dessert portion

Sesame Pasta Salad

Here's a delicious recipe created by M. Caraluzzi of the American Cafe in Baltimore and Washington, D.C.

    1 lb. whole-wheat spaghetti or flat noodles
    ¼ cup sesame oil
    3 Tbsp. tamari
    1 clove garlic, chopped
    freshly ground pepper
    ½ red pepper, diced fine
    ¼ cup watercress, chopped

    Cook pasta according to package directions. Do not overcook. Drain quickly and submerge in cold water and drain again. Mix in the sesame oil, tamari, garlic, and pepper at once. Gently fold in the red pepper and watercress.
    Serves 8 as a side dish.

Each serving is made up of: 1 Grain portion
                           ½ Healthful Dessert portion

Whole-Wheat Bread

    6 cups whole-wheat flour
    1 package active dry yeast
    1 tsp. salt (optional)
    2 cups water
    ¼ cup safflower oil
    2 Tbsp. honey

Mix 2 cups of the flour with yeast and salt. Heat water and oil together until warm (105°–115°). Add honey and stir into flour. Beat well. Mix in enough of the remaining flour to make a soft dough that leaves the side of the bowl. Knead on a lightly floured surface until dough is smooth and elastic, about 15 minutes. Place dough in a greased bowl and turn over once to grease upper side of dough. Cover and let rise in a warm place (80°–85°) until double in size, about 1 hour. Grease two 9 × 5 × 3 loaf pans. Press dough down to remove air bubbles. Divide dough in half, shape, and place in pans. Cover and let rise in a warm place until double in size, about 50 minutes. Place in preheated 375° oven. Bake until bread sounds hollow when tapped, about 30 minutes. Remove bread from pans and cool on rack.

Servings: 16 slices per loaf.

Each serving is made up of: 1½ Grain portions
½ Healthful Dessert portion

Fiesta Pasta Picnic Salad

2 lbs. macaroni, any tube type, such as rigatoni or penni, preferably whole-wheat
2 Tbsp. olive oil
4 cloves of garlic, minced
1½ cups tomatoes, peeled, seeded, and roughly chopped
¾ cup part-skim mozzarella cheese, cut in cubes
6 black olives, rinsed and cut in half
2 Tbsp. chopped parsley
3 Tbsp. red wine or tarragon vinegar
freshly ground black pepper, to taste

Cook pasta according to package directions, making sure not to overcook. While pasta is cooking, heat oil in small saucepan, add garlic, and sauté. Do not brown. Add tomatoes for a few seconds, stirring, until *barely* heated. Take off heat and cool. Combine with well drained pasta, cheese, olives, parsley, red wine or vinegar, and pepper. Toss.

Serves 10.

Note: A can of water-packed low-sodium tuna, flaked, or a

cup of cubed cooked chicken may be added to this dish.

Each serving is made up of: 1 Grain portion
1 Healthful Dessert portion
1 Dairy portion
1 Vegetable portion

Risotto alla Milanese

This is an adaptation of a classic Italian dish. Prepared with brown rice it will have a crunchy consistency rather than a creamy one. Also, brown rice requires longer cooking and more liquid, so be prepared with a bit more stock. The dish is marvelous "as is," but you can make it a meal-in-one by adding a cup of cooked chicken, turkey, shrimp, or meat at the end and heating it through.

½ cup chopped onions
2 Tbsp. olive oil
1½ cups uncooked short-grain brown rice
¼ cup of Marsala wine (optional)
4–5 cups strong, hot chicken or vegetable stock, either
  homemade or low-sodium
⅛ tsp. powdered saffron
½ tsp. white pepper
½ cup part-skim mozzarella cheese, cut in small cubes
salt substitute (optional) and pepper to taste
1 Tbsp. Parmesan cheese, grated

In a large skillet cook onions in olive oil 2 to 3 minutes until transparent. Stir in rice with a fork. Add wine at this point if using. Add 2 cups of hot stock to rice and continue stirring. Add saffron. Add more stock as liquid is absorbed. This process will take about 30 minutes. When all the liquid is absorbed and the rice tastes tender and crunchy, add mozzarella bit by bit. Season with salt, pepper, and Parmesan cheese.

Serves 6.

Each serving is made up of: 3 Grain portions
1 Healthful Dessert portion
1 Dairy portion

Polenta, Plain and Fancy

Polenta is the staff of life in many parts of Italy, for breakfast and with variations at other meals. Try the variation described here as a luncheon dish or a dinner accompaniment. Delicious!

6½ cups water
2 cups coarse-grained cornmeal
Vegit to taste
white pepper, to taste
½ cup tomato sauce
¼ cup Parmesan cheese, grated

Bring water to a boil and turn down to simmer. Begin adding cornmeal in a *very thin stream* (to prevent lumping), stirring constantly with a wooden spoon. Continue stirring after all the cornmeal has been added. The polenta is done when it pulls away from the sides of the pan. Season to taste. Pour the polenta onto a large platter and flatten with a spatula; a wooden one works best. (You may have to dip the spatula in cold water to flatten evenly.) Allow to cool. Cut the polenta in rounds or squares and place overlapping slices in a baking dish that has been lightly oiled with olive oil. Top with ½ cup tomato sauce and sprinkle with Parmesan cheese. Bake in preheated 350° oven for 10 to 15 minutes, until browned on top.

Serves 6.

Each serving is made up of: 1½ Grain portions

Pasta Gretchen

2 lbs. fresh tomatoes, cut in cubes, seeded, not peeled
5 black olives, rinsed and sliced
2 oz. mozzarella cheese, cubed
1 3½-oz. can Italian tuna fish (see note)
2 tsp. oil from the tuna
2 Tbsp. olive oil
½ cup fresh basil, chopped
½ cup parsley, chopped
2 cloves garlic, chopped
seasoning herbs (Vegit)
½ lb. angel hair or other thin pasta, preferably whole-wheat
2 Tbsp. Parmesan cheese, grated

Heat chopped garlic in 1 tablespoon of olive oil. Place tomatoes, olives, mozzarella cheese, tuna fish, tuna oil, remaining olive oil, basil, parsley, and garlic in a large bowl and allow to stand for at least one hour. Add seasoning herbs to taste.

Cook pasta according to package directions, making certain not to overcook. The pasta should be just barely done, or it will be mushy. Drain pasta and add reserved sauce. Top with Parmesan cheese.

Serves 4.

Note: If Italian tuna is not available, use regular water-packed tuna and add two teaspoons of oil to recipe. Italian tuna is packed in olive oil.

Each serving is made up of: 1 Grain portion
2 Healthful Dessert portions
1 Protein portion
2 Dairy portions
1 Vegetable portion

Pasta and Clam Sauce

5 lbs. baby clams
2 Tbsp. olive oil
2 cloves of garlic, chopped
3 sprigs of parsley, chopped
1 lb. ripe tomatoes, peeled and coarsely chopped
freshly ground pepper
Vegit, to taste
1¼ lbs. whole-wheat pasta

Wash and scrub clams and soak in cold water for half an hour to allow the remaining sand to fall to the bottom of the pan. Rinse in a colander. Heat oil in large pot and add the garlic and parsley. Sauté for about 2 minutes and add tomatoes. Season. Raise heat to medium and cook for another 15 minutes.

Cook pasta according to package directions. Add clams to pot, cover, lower heat, and cook for 10 minutes or until the shells open. Serve over drained pasta.

Serves 6.

Each serving is made up of: 1½ Grain portions
1 Healthful Dessert portion
2 Protein portions
1 Vegetable portion

Lentil Salad

2 cups dried lentils
4 cups water
2 Tbsp. olive oil
4 Tbsp. white wine vinegar or lemon juice
freshly ground pepper
½ tsp. light soy sauce or tamari
⅓ cup scallions or chives, finely chopped

Rinse and pick over lentils. Boil in water until tender, about 40 minutes. Drain and cool.

Mix oil with vinegar or lemon juice, pepper, and soy sauce with a wire whisk until well blended. Pour over lentils while they are still warm. Fold in chives or scallions and marinate several hours before serving. Add additional oil if necessary.

May be made ahead and refrigerated. Take out an hour before serving. Serve at room temperature.

Serves 6.

Each serving is made up of: 1 Grain portion
1 Healthful Dessert portion

Hummus (Bean Dip)

2 cups drained and rinsed canned chick-peas (garbanzos)
¼ cup fresh lemon juice
1 Tbsp. chopped garlic
2 Tbsp. chopped parsley
freshly ground pepper
dash of salt (optional)

Spread well-drained chick-peas on paper towels and pat dry. Combine chick-peas, lemon juice, garlic, parsley, pepper, and salt in blender or food processor and blend for about 30 seconds. With machine off, scrape down sides and blend again. The consistency should be thick enough to hold its shape on a spoon. If Hummus seems too bland, add more lemon juice or a dash of low-sodium soy sauce.

Serve with sesame crackers and/or vegetable sticks.
Serves 18: 2 tablespoons per serving.

Each serving is made up of: 1 Grain portion

Shirley's Bran Muffins

2 or 3 small or medium apples, cored, not peeled and
  cut in small pieces
3 eggs
¼ cup water
½ tsp. nutmeg
1 tsp. baking soda
1 tsp. baking powder
1 tsp. vanilla extract
1 tsp. cinnamon
¼ tsp. almond extract (optional)
2 cups unprocessed bran (either wheat or oat)

Combine apples, eggs, water, nutmeg, baking soda, baking powder, vanilla, cinnamon, and almond extract in a blender or food processor. After blending, pour contents into a bowl and stir in 2 cups of bran. Coat 12 muffin tins with safflower oil and spoon mixture into tins. Bake at 400° for 20 minutes.
Serves 12.
Note: Muffins should be refrigerated if not used at once. May also be frozen.

Each serving is made up of: ¼ Fruit portion
                            ½ Grain portion

Pumpkin Nut Muffins

1 cup walnuts, chopped
1½ cups whole-wheat pastry flour
½ tsp. salt (optional)
½ tsp. cinnamon
½ tsp. nutmeg
1 tsp. baking powder
1 tsp. baking soda
2 Tbsp. sesame oil
¼ cup honey
1 egg
½ cup water
½ cup raisins
1 cup pumpkin, finely grated

Roast walnuts lightly in 250° oven. Sift flour with salt, cinnamon, nutmeg, baking powder, and baking soda.

In bowl blend sesame oil, honey, egg, and water. Add roasted walnuts and raisins, then add grated pumpkin. Cut in flour with a pastry blender until just mixed. Grease 12 muffin tins and fill almost full with batter. Bake at 400° for approximately 20 minutes.

Serves 12.

Each serving is made up of: 1 Grain portion
½ Healthful Dessert portion

Blueberry Muffins

1½ cups water
3 cups rolled oats
1 cup whole-wheat pastry flour
1 tsp. baking soda
½ tsp. salt (optional)
1 Tbsp. honey
½ cup raisins, blueberries, or chopped almonds

Combine water, oats, flour, baking soda, salt, honey, and the ½ cup raisins, blueberries, or almonds. Stir together. Drop by tablespoons into 12 lightly oiled muffin cups. Bake at 400° for 20 minutes.

Serves 12.

Each serving is made up of: 1 Fruit portion
1 Grain portion

Cranberry Bread

2 cups whole-wheat pastry flour
2 cups unbleached white flour
1 Tbsp. baking powder
1 tsp. baking soda
1 tsp. salt (optional)
½ tsp. cinnamon
¼ tsp. nutmeg
½ cup sesame oil
1 Tbsp. grated orange rind
1½ cup orange juice, fresh
1 cup maple syrup
2 cups cranberries, fresh or frozen, unsweetened
1 cup chopped walnuts
⅔ cup raisins

Preheat oven to 350°.
Sift together the flours, baking powder, baking soda, salt (if using), cinnamon, and nutmeg. Add oil and stir in thoroughly. In a separate bowl combine orange rind, orange juice, and maple syrup. Add to flour-oil mixture. Fold in berries, nuts, and raisins. Divide batter and turn into two greased and floured 9×5 loaf pans. Bake at 350° 55 to 60 minutes. Cool and refrigerate. Slices better the next day.
Yields 2 loaves, 16 slices per loaf.

Each serving is made up of: 1 Fruit portion
1 Grain portion

Golden Sauerkraut and Noodles

1 cup sauerkraut, packed tightly (use low-sodium, if obtainable)
2 Tbsp. olive oil
1 small onion, about ¼ cup chopped
¼ lb. medium-width whole-wheat noodles
½ tsp. caraway seeds
¼ cup fresh peas (optional)

Drain and rinse sauerkraut thoroughly to remove brine,
thus removing high sodium content. Squeeze small handfuls
at a time to remove as much moisture as possible. Spread on
paper towels to dry.

In a 10-inch skillet quickly sauté onions in one tablespoon
of oil until golden. Do not brown. Set aside. Cook noodles in
unsalted water until barely done. Do not overcook. Drain and
set aside.

Replace skillet on range. Turn heat to medium. Add re-
maining oil. Carefully separate sauerkraut and add to skillet.
Carefully separate the noodles in the same manner and add
to skillet. Stir together and cook quickly until almost crisp.
Add caraway seeds and peas, stir, and heat through and serve.
Serves 2.

Each serving is made up of: 1 Grain portion
½ Healthful Dessert portion
1 Vegetable portion

VEGETABLES

Warm Beet Salad

1 doz. small to medium beets
Yogurt Dijon Salad Dressing (see recipe pages 139–140)
fresh chives or ½ onion, thinly sliced
Dark leaf lettuce

Wash beets and cut off tops, leaving about 1 inch. Place beets in large saucepan and cover halfway with water. Bring to a boil and cook until beets are tender, about half an hour. When cool, skin and cut beets in quarters. Lightly toss with dressing. Sprinkle with chives or onions and serve on a bed of lettuce.

Serves 6.

Note: Any leftover beets may be added to a green salad.

Each serving is made up of: 1½ Vegetable portions

Escarole Braised with Garlic

Escarole is a wonderful green for salads, but is just as tasty when cooked as a vegetable, especially in oil and garlic. It's so simple and quick to prepare, too.

1 large head of escarole
2 Tbsp. olive oil
2 cloves of garlic, crushed or chopped
freshly ground pepper

Cut off the bottom of the escarole and separate the leaves. Cut them in halves or thirds. Wash leaves and put them in a large skillet with a cover. (Do not shake off the water after washing.) The water on the leaves will be enough to cook the vegetable. Cook escarole over medium heat until tender, about 10 minutes. Drain, saving the water for stock.
Heat olive oil in the same pan and sauté the garlic for a minute or two. Add the drained escarole and turn in the pan several times until heated through. Season with pepper.

Serves 4.

Each serving is made up of: ½ Healthful Dessert portion
½ Vegetable portion

Baked Zucchini

¾ lb. (about 2 cups) zucchini, unpeeled and thickly sliced
1 Tbsp. whole-wheat flour
freshly ground pepper to taste
Vegit to taste
2 Tbsp. olive oil
1 clove garlic, finely minced
3 Tbsp. fresh basil, chopped
3 Tbsp. Parmesan cheese, grated

Preheat oven to 400°.
Dry zucchini slices on paper towels. Combine flour with pepper and Vegit and toss with the zucchini in a brown paper bag. Heat oil in oven-proof skillet or casserole and add zucchini, tossing occasionally and taking care not to break up slices. You may have to do this in two batches. When the zucchini are golden brown add garlic and basil, sprinkle cheese over the top, and bake 5 minutes.
Serves 4.

Each serving is made up of: ¾ Healthful Dessert portion
1 Vegetable portion

Zucchini and Tomato Italian Style

1½ Tbsp. olive oil
1 medium onion, thinly sliced
1 clove garlic, minced
1 medium zucchini, thinly sliced
1 medium tomato, seeded and cut in chunks
½ tsp. dried basil
salt substitute
freshly ground pepper

Heat oil in large skillet. Add onions and garlic and cook for 2 minutes. Add sliced zucchini and sauté until zucchini begins to turn brown around edges. Add tomatoes and basil, stir and cook for 2 to 3 minutes. Add seasonings to taste.

Cover pan. Turn off heat and let stand for a few minutes to allow flavors to blend.

Serves 3.

Each serving is made up of: ½ Healthful Dessert portion
1¼ Vegetable portions

Carrots Raspberry

2 large or 3 medium carrots
2 Tbsp. water
1 Tbsp. unsalted butter
1 Tbsp. lemon juice
1 tsp. raspberry vinegar
½ Tbsp. honey

Peel and thinly slice carrots. In small covered saucepan, place carrots with 2 tablespoons of water and butter. Bring to a high heat and quickly lower heat. Cook 10 minutes or until just done. Watch carefully that the carrots don't burn. Add lemon juice, raspberry vinegar, and honey. Stir. Turn off heat. Shake pan with cover on and allow flavors to blend for 2 minutes and serve.

Serves 2.

Each serving is made up of: 1 Vegetable portion

Spicy Wok Broccoli

1 large bunch of broccoli
3 Tbsp. sesame oil
2 tsp. ginger, grated
3 cloves garlic, minced
1 large onion, chopped
1 lb. tofu, firm style
2 scallions, slivered
1 cup peanuts, coarsely chopped
2 Tbsp. light soy sauce

Cut off bottom of broccoli stems and discard; coarsely chop the rest. Heat wok or heavy skillet with the oil. Add ginger, garlic, and onions and cook for one minute. Add tofu and stir-fry on high for about 8 to 10 minutes. Set this mixture aside on warmed plate. Add broccoli, scallions, peanuts, and soy sauce to the wok and continue to stir-fry until the broccoli is bright green, about 3 to 4 minutes. Combine mixtures. Serve over rice or rice noodles.
Serves 6.

Each serving is made up of: 2 Healthful Dessert portions
                          2 Protein portions
                          1 Vegetable portion

Braised Celery

A wonderful way to get the fiber you need from a cooked vegetable.

1 large bunch of celery
½ cup homemade chicken or vegetable stock, or canned
  low-sodium stock
2 Tbsp. butter, unsalted
½ tsp. fennel seeds
Vegit to taste

Clean celery. (Reserve green tops for soup.) Cut celery stalks in 2-inch diagonal lengths. In saucepan or skillet with a tight-fitting lid place celery, stock, butter, fennel, and seasoning. Cover pan and simmer a half-hour or until vegetable is tender. Correct seasoning, if necessary.
Serves 4.

Each serving is made up of: ½ Healthful Dessert portion
                          ½ Vegetable portion

Paul's Potatoes

¼ Tbsp. olive oil per person
1 medium potato per person

Coat surface of nonstick baking pan with olive oil. (Pan size depends on number of potatoes.) Wash potatoes and slice* about ¼ inch thick. Lay in single layer in pan. Bake at 350° until well browned.

*Potatoes may be cut French-style, shoestring, or, if you can cut them thin enough, into potato chips.

1 potato per serving.

Each serving is made up of: 1 Grain portion

Autumn Casserole

1 large onion, sliced
1 Tbsp. olive oil
2 carrots, sliced
1 large parsnip, sliced
3 small potatoes, peeled and sliced
2 sweet potatoes, peeled and sliced
½ rutabaga, peeled and sliced
1 turnip, sliced
2 cups red cabbage, sliced
1 large apple, peeled and sliced
½ cup walnuts, chopped

Sauté onions in oil until soft. In a shallow-lidded baking dish, place consecutive layers of onions, vegetables, and apple. Repeat until dish is filled. Add water to cover bottom of dish. Don't let casserole get too dry. Bake covered at 400° about 30 to 45 minutes until very soft. Remove lid, sprinkle with nuts, return to oven, and bake until nuts are brown.

Serves 6.

Each serving is made up of: 1½ Grain portions
1 Healthful Dessert portion
1 Vegetable portion

SAUCES AND SALAD DRESSINGS

Strawberry Sauce

1 pint of strawberries*
2 Tbsp. honey
2 Tbsp. fruit liqueur (optional)

Clean berries and cut in half. (There should be about 2 cups.) Place berries in blender or food processor with honey and blend. Add liqueur and blend again. Serve on griddle cakes, gelatin, gingerbread.
Serves 8.
Note: You may replace strawberries with raspberries. Out of season, use frozen berries to equal 2 cups.

Each serving is made up of: 1 Fruit portion

Tomato Sauce

2 Tbsp. olive oil
2 large onions, coarsely chopped
2 small carrots, coarsely chopped
4 cloves of garlic, chopped
1 2-lb., 3-oz. can Italian plum tomatoes
2 tsp. dried oregano
2 Tbsp. fresh, or 2 tsp. dried, basil
freshly ground pepper to taste

Heat oil in large pot. Add onions, carrots, and garlic, and sauté until vegetables are golden brown. Put the tomatoes through a sieve, pushing pulp through with a wooden spoon. Discard the seeds. Add seasoning to the pot and partly cover and simmer for 30 minutes. Purée in a blender or food processor.
Yield: 6 cups.

Each serving is made up of: 1 Healthful Dessert portion
2½ Vegetable portions

Mayonnaise

This no-yolk mayonnaise can be whipped up in seconds in a blender and refrigerated. The taste can be varied by adding minced garlic (about a ½ teaspoon) for a lovely flavoring with fish, or a ¼ cup chopped parsley or basil for a pasta dressing. It's delicious, but please use it sparingly.

> 2 large egg whites
> 1 tsp. Dijon mustard
> Vegit, dash
> white pepper, to taste
> ½ cup safflower oil
> ¼ cup olive oil
> 1 Tbsp. fresh lemon juice

In blender place the egg whites, mustard, Vegit, and pepper, and run blender at low speed for about 1 minute. Combine oils and, with motor running, add oils slowly in a thin stream. Turn motor off and add lemon juice. Blend again until thick and creamy. Taste. Add more lemon juice if needed. Refrigerate.

Yields about 17 tablespoons.

Each serving is made up of: 1 Healthful Dessert portion

Dijon Salad Dressing

> 2 Tbsp. olive oil, extra virgin, if possible
> 1 Tbsp. white or red wine vinegar, or fresh lemon juice
> ⅛ tsp. balsamic vinegar (optional)
> 1 tsp. Dijon mustard
> ½ tsp. dried Italian salad herbs
> ⅛ tsp. garlic, minced
> freshly ground pepper

Blend all ingredients with a wire whisk and pour over salad.

You may substitute 1 tablespoon of low-fat plain yogurt for 1 tablespoon of olive oil. In this case, use the lemon juice instead of vinegar.

Serves 4.

Each serving is made up of: ½ Healthful Dessert portion

Linseed Oil Dressing

Developed by Mrs. Joan Rudin and Dr. Donald Rudin, this dressing is highly recommended. Please be certain to use only linseed (flaxseed) oil obtainable only at health-food stores, and not the kind from hardware stores. Always refrigerate linseed oil.

1 cup linseed oil (flaxseed)
⅓ cup vinegar
1 Tbsp. Dijon-type mustard
1 tsp. tamari
1 Tbsp. crushed, dried basil

Combine all ingredients and beat with a wire whisk or place in a jar with a tight cover and shake. *Always* refrigerate unprocessed oils.

Serves 20; each serving equals two tablespoons.

Each serving is made up of: 1 Healthful Dessert portion

Black Bean Sauce

1 small onion, chopped
2 celery stalks, chopped
1 clove garlic
2 Tbsp. olive oil
1 tsp. oregano
1½ tsp. fresh grated ginger
juice of one lemon
2 cups cooked black beans

Sauté onion, celery, and garlic in oil. Stir in oregano and ginger. Add beans and lightly stir at medium heat. Add lemon juice and enough water to just cover. Bring to a boil. Put mixture in blender and blend at high speed until smooth. Serve over rice, noodles, or millet.

Serves 8.

Each serving is made up of: ½ Grain portion
½ Vegetable portion

Sweet-and-Sour Sauce

1½ cups unsweetened pineapple juice
½ cup plus 2 Tbsp. maple syrup
½ cup apple cider vinegar
¼ tsp. garlic powder
2 Tbsp. arrowroot

Combine juice, syrup, cider vinegar, garlic powder, and arrowroot in a saucepan over medium heat. Whisk out all lumps and beat, stirring constantly until thickened. Use over fish or chicken.

Makes 8 ¼-cup servings.

Each serving is made up of: 2 Fruit portions

Oriental Marinade

¼ cup dry sherry
¼ cup tamari, low-sodium
¼ cup vinegar
1 tsp. prepared mustard
2 cloves garlic, mashed
2 tsp. fresh grated ginger
1 tsp. honey
2 Tbsp. fresh lemon juice
1 Tbsp. sesame oil
1 Tbsp. olive oil
pinch cayenne

Place all ingredients in a tightly sealed jar and shake well. Use as a marinade for chicken, fish, or tofu. Marinate for one hour or overnight. Drain off marinade and broil the chicken, fish, or tofu.

Note: Since this marinade is drained, most of the calories and sodium are not retained.

2 Tbsp. per serving.

Each serving is made up of: ½ Healthful Dessert portion

DESSERTS

Sugar-free Gelatin

1 qt. fruit juice (any kind except citrus or pineapple)
½ tsp. cinnamon
2 packets plain gelatin
2 cups fresh fruit, chopped

Bring juice and cinnamon to a boil. Add gelatin and cook 5 minutes. Lay chopped fruit in the bottom of a 9 × 11 flat baking dish and pour gelatin mixture over it. Let cool and refrigerate until firm.

Serves 12.

Each serving is made up of: 1 Fruit portion

Indian Pudding

1 qt. skim milk
1 cup cornmeal
1 egg
1 tsp. salt (optional)
½ tsp. ginger
½ tsp. nutmeg
2 Tbsp. oil
⅓ cup maple syrup or honey
½ cup raisins (optional)
1 tsp. vanilla

Combine all ingredients, stir together, and place in a casserole dish. Place dish in a larger pan of water and bake at 375° for 25 minutes.
Serves 8.

Each serving is made up of: 1 Fruit portion
                                            1 Grain portion
                                            ½ Dairy portion

Apple Raisin Crisp

Topping
2 cups rolled oats
¼ tsp. salt
⅓ cup oil
½ cup honey

Mix oats, salt, and nuts together. Add oil and mix well. Add honey and mix to coat all ingredients.

Crisp
6 apples, cored and sliced
1 cup raisins
1 cup apple juice
¼ tsp. salt (optional)
1½ Tbsp. arrowroot (cornstarch) diluted in ¼ cup water
½ tsp. cinnamon
½ tsp. vanilla

Arrange sliced apples in a baking dish and set aside. Cook raisins in 1 cup apple juice with salt, if using, until soft. Thicken with diluted arrowroot. Sprinkle cinnamon and vanilla on apples, then pour on raisin sauce. Cover with topping. Bake at 350° for 40 minutes.
Serves 12.

Each serving is made up of: 1 Fruit portion
                                            1 Grain portion
                                            1 Healthful Dessert portion

Banana/Strawberry "Ice Cream"

4 large bananas, very ripe
2 cups strawberries, cleaned and hulled

Freeze the bananas whole. Pare off skins with a knife and discard. Chop into small pieces and place in blender or food processor. Add strawberries. Begin at slow speed and add drops of water, enough to allow process. When completely whipped empty into freezer container and freeze until ready to serve.

Note: You may substitute raspberries or pineapple for the strawberries.

Serves 6.

Each serving is made up of: 2 Fruit portions

Accidental Mousse

This delicious dessert is a natural! No sugar or sweeteners added.

1½ cups unsweetened applesauce
6 very ripe medium bananas, peeled and cut in quarters
2 Tbsp. carob powder
¼ tsp. vanilla extract

In a food processor, using the steel blade, blend the applesauce and bananas, adding bananas one piece at a time. Add carob powder and vanilla. Continue to blend until the mixture is smooth and all the bananas have been blended with no chunks remaining. Spoon into individual dessert cups and refrigerate for 30 minutes.

Serves 8.

Each serving is made up of: 2 Fruit portions

Mustard Gingerbread

2½ cups whole-wheat pastry flour
1½ tsp. baking powder
½ tsp. salt (optional)
½ cup safflower oil
½ tsp. baking soda
½ tsp. cloves
1 tsp. powdered mustard
1 tsp. cinnamon
1 cup hot water
1 tsp. fresh grated ginger
1 tsp. powdered ginger
1 cup molasses
1 large egg

Sift together flour, baking powder, and salt (if desired). To the safflower oil add baking soda, cloves, mustard, cinnamon, grated ginger, and powdered ginger. Beat in molasses and egg. Add flour mixture alternately with hot water. Beat for 30 seconds. Turn into a well-greased and floured 9″ bread pan. Bake at 350° for 45 minutes. Cool for 10 minutes. Serve with Crême de Cream (see below).
Yields 16 slices.

Each serving is made up of: 1 Grain portion
                             1¼ Healthful Dessert portions

Crême de Cream

1 cup cold skim milk
½ cup powdered skim milk
1 Tbsp. vegetable, almond, or walnut oil

Pour the fresh milk into blender at high speed. Add powdered milk a tablespoon at a time. Slowly add vegetable oil. Use at once or freeze. Use on gingerbread or other dessert.
Serves 6, 2 tablespoons per serving.

Each serving is made up of: ¾ Dairy portion

Tofu Whipped Cream

2 cups tofu
½ cup oil, either sesame or walnut
⅓ cup plus 2 Tbsp. honey
1¼ tsp. vanilla
1 Tbsp. plus 1 tsp. lemon juice
3 Tbsp. soy milk

Blend together all the ingredients, and chill for one hour before serving. This is an excellent nondairy topping.
Makes 12 servings, ¼ cup each.

Each serving is made up of: 1 Healthful Dessert portion
1 Protein portion

Mary Theresa's Corn Shortcake

1½ cups cornmeal
1½ cups whole-wheat pastry flour
1 tsp. baking powder
½ tsp. cinnamon
⅓ cup sesame oil
¼ tsp. tamari
½ cup water
½ cup apple juice
¼ cup maple syrup or honey

Preheat oven to 350°.
Mix cornmeal, flour, baking powder, and cinnamon together in a bowl. With fingers rub the sesame oil into this mixture until all the oil is absorbed. In second bowl combine the tamari, water, apple juice, and maple syrup or honey. Add this mixture to the flour mixture and turn the whole into an oiled 7 × 7 baking pan. Bake for 40 minutes.
Serve with Strawberry Sauce (see page 138).
Serves 9.

Each serving is made up of: 1½ Grain portions
1 Healthful Dessert portion

Velvet Pumpkin Cream Pie

1 1/2 cups cooked pumpkin
1/2 cup maple syrup
2 tsp. orange juice
1 1/2 cups water
1 tsp. cinnamon
1/2 tsp. fresh ginger, grated
1/2 tsp. nutmeg
1 tsp. vanilla
2 eggs
pinch of salt (optional)

In blender blend pumpkin with maple syrup. Add orange juice, water, cinnamon, ginger, nutmeg, vanilla, eggs, and salt (if desired) and blend well until smooth and creamy. (This may have to be mixed in a bowl first and poured into blender in 2 or 3 batches.) Pour into pie crust; try the Flaky Pie Crust following. Bake at 375° for 45 minutes.
Serves 6.

Each serving is made up of: 1/2 Grain portion
1 Healthful Dessert portion

Flaky Pie Crust (for 2 pies)

1 cup oat flour
2 cups whole-wheat pastry flour
1 Tbsp. arrowroot
1/2 cup butter
1/3 tsp. salt

Place flours and salt in a bowl. Grate butter into mixture and blend. Add water to form into a ball. Roll dough out to 1/4" thick. Bake at 375° for 8 to 10 minutes.
Serves 8.

Each serving is made up of: 2 Healthful Dessert portions

MISCELLANEOUS

Green Drink

A quick pick-me-up and kids love it!

> 2 cups fresh spinach, or combine with mint, parsley, or
>   other greens
> 1½ cups pineapple juice

Blend ingredients at high speed for 15 seconds.
Serves 4.

Each serving is made up of: 1 Fruit portion
                             1 Vegetable portion

Fruit Jam

> ½ lb. dried fruit. Choose from dried apricots, dried
>   peaches, dried apples, pitted prunes or raisins, or com-
>   bine two or more to make ½ pound .
> 2 cups water*
> ginger or cinnamon, powdered, to taste

In a saucepan cook the fruit with 1½ cups of water until
plump and juicy. Purée in a blender to make a smooth paste.
Add seasoning to taste. Add remaining water and blend. Store
in refrigerator.
    Yields 2½ cups. Serving size: 2 tablespoons.
    *You may replace part of the water with fruit juice.

Each serving is made up of: 1 Healthful Dessert portion

HOW TO ASSERT YOURSELF IN A RESTAURANT

The time is not too distant when restaurants will serve whole-wheat breads, offer brown rice in place of white, and include whole grains in place of refined flour products in their daily fare. But until then you are going to have to learn to be discriminating in the choice of foods you order when dining out.

Assertiveness training is in order if you have any desire to eat healthfully at a restaurant. It's very easy to quickly survey the menu, see what is offered, and order with the request that the sauces be omitted. Broiled fish or chicken, steamed vegetables, salads with oil and vinegar or a vinaigrette dressing, and fresh fruits for dessert will serve you well.

French

French food will no longer challenge your faithfulness to your food program now that nouvelle cuisine is the fashionable way to eat. Rich creamy sauces, once the mainstay of French cooking, are out. Light fare is in. Hors d'oeuvres need not be high in fats. Pâté is not the order of the day. No, the order is for a simple melon, leeks in vinaigrette, a plate of oysters, mussels, or any seasonal seafood. Entrées can be a steaming bowl of bouillabaisse; poached, baked, or broiled fish or chicken. The French serve the most marvelous green salads . . . mixed endive, watercress, and other attractive leafy wonders in a simple vinaigrette dressing. For dessert nothing matches a plate of fresh strawberries or raspberries, perhaps with a dash of champagne, or a lovely sorbet. Avoid the temptation to disguise your vegetable or entrée in rich cream or butter sauces. Skip the hollandaise, the mousse, the pâté, and the bisques on the menu. You'll find plenty to eat within the limits of your food plan the fashionable French way.

Italian

Pasta is perfect on the Bio-Nutrionics Food Plan, so eating in an Italian restaurant presents no problem. Here you can begin your meal with a hearty minestrone, or one of the many pasta dishes that are so delicious: spaghetti with a light fresh tomato-and-basil sauce or a primavera sauce are just some suggestions. Linguine with clam sauce, red or white, or a mixed seafood sauce if you prefer. For an entrée, the Italian way with chicken and fish is usually appropriate. Ask that the dish be cooked simply in olive oil and not butter. And don't reach for the garlic bread!

Desserts in an Italian restaurant are limited, but you can enjoy various forms of fresh fruit.

Mexican

Mexican food has finally found a place in the American palate and restaurants are springing up all around us offering the succulent, nourishing repasts from south of the border. Here's where you can indulge your taste for marvelously flavored bean and corn dishes. The bean and lentil soups are high in protein and wonderful, filling "starters," as the English call the first course. For the main course you have a choice of burritos, chicken enchilada, or tamale, arroz con pollo, or any chicken, fish, or seafood dish with rice. Ask the kitchen not to top your serving of burritos, enchiladas, or tamales with cheese, guacamole, or sour cream, and discard the skin on the chicken. You will also have to avoid munching on nachos or dipping the corn chips in guacamole sauce. Dip the chips in salsa instead.

Chinese

The Chinese menu is perhaps the easiest to order from, with its variety of foods that are rich in vegetables and scant in cholesterol. If you're not in the mood for chicken or fish, here's your chance to indulge your taste for beef prepared the stir-fry way, as there's little beef used in this cooking method. Other wonders of the Chinese kitchen that will satisfy your taste buds are lemon chicken, ginger fish, and vegetables with peanuts or cashews. The items to avoid are the deep-fried foods, such as fried wonton, spare ribs, and any of the pork dishes.

Let common sense be your guide when ordering and don't let yourself be influenced by headwaiters or fellow diners who overindulge. If you want to lower your cholesterol, you must take control of every facet of your life.

6. Physical Activity

ADD PHYSICAL ACTIVITY TO NUTRITION FOR FAST RESULTS

The Bio-Nutrionics Nutrition Plan will work by itself to reduce saturated fat intake and cholesterol, but it will work much more efficiently in combination with a regular program of physical activity. During exercise, oxygen is brought into your body to nourish every cell. It causes you to perspire and to eliminate waste and impurities through your skin. Activity increases circulation, respiration, and your energy level. The calories burned during movement help you obtain and maintain your desired weight, body tone, and shape. It enhances your overall sense of well-being. All the benefits can be obtained at nearly any age, a fact demonstrated by studies that have measured the effects of exercise on the heart, lungs, bones, skin, and the brain.

For instance, a Mississippi research group in a report to the Scientific Sessions of the American Heart Association in Washington, D.C., in November 1985, claimed that regular aerobic exercise may help lower mild high blood pressure without medication. In their research a group of healthy middle-aged men performed a half-hour of moderate aerobic exercises three times a week. Another group did nonaerobic exercises for the same amount of time. After ten weeks the aerobically trained group averaged a 10-millimeter reduction in their diastolic blood pressure. (That's the lower of the two numbers in a blood pressure reading.)

Studies also prove that people who exercise increase their HDLs (the good cholesterol). The difference in serum HDL between highly active people and less active people varies between 15 percent and 50 percent, with the more active people having higher HDLs. This difference was observed for the first time in skiers, runners, and lumberjacks. The research supports the premise that frequent, regular physical activity is beneficial to the heart and helps improve the ratio of HDL to LDL cholesterol.

GET UP AND GET ACTIVE

Before the days of cholesterol overload our ancestors raised their own food and earned their livelihood being physically active. For most of us, life is not like that. The longest daily walk many of us take today is from the house to the car in the driveway, and from the parking lot to the supermarket or the office. The time has come to get up and get active!

We don't really care for the word "exercise." It implies jumping around in one fashion or another—running, jogging, aerobic dancing, skipping—any one of a number of exercise regimens that put a sudden strain on long-unused muscles. It stands to reason that if you've been sitting immobilized for most of your waking hours you can't suddenly take up jogging for thirty minutes a day, and we don't expect you to. You'll succeed only in traumatizing your joints. But to gain the most from this program you must become more active. It's easy . . . just choose something that gets you to move, even if it's chopping wood, dancing, gardening, or bowling (see our suggestions on pages 157 and 158). You may prefer the companionship offered by health clubs or wish to make an outing like biking or hiking a family activity. Whatever you pick, make sure it fits into your life-style and doesn't become a chore.

Also, don't set your goals too high; that's unrealistic. Match the vigor of your activity program with your present physical condition or you will quickly become overwhelmed. Begin slowly, for instance, by walking around the block in the fresh air during your lunch hour. The fresh air and sunshine will do you good. Remember, choosing an activity you'll stick with is the key to your success. We know you can do it!

THE REMARKABLE BENEFITS OF WALKING

What do you think is the best exercise? Is it jogging, running, mountain climbing, bicycling, or walking? The answer may surprise you. The more strenuous exercises like jogging, running, and mountain climbing don't seem to be more beneficial to the heart than a regular schedule of brisk walking. Doctors at Duke University Medical Center report that walking favorably alters cholesterol levels; lowers blood sugar, insulin, and triglycerides; and helps you to lose weight or maintain ideal weight. It also reduces stress, strengthens leg and abdominal muscles, and increases cardiovascular endurance. You gain all these benefits as long as you walk regularly.

Set Your Own Pace

Start slowly and gradually extend your walking program both in the time you spend at it and in the degree of exertion. One block will soon become five, five will become ten, and the time it takes you to complete your course will shorten eventually. Let your first goal be a twenty- to twenty-five-minute mile and then try and lower your time. The pace at which you walk is not really too important, however. Walking briskly is better, but walking two or three miles a day three or four days a week can be just what the doctor ordered. No doubt about it, walking is one exercise we recommend unequivocally. It's hard to perform incorrectly and it's not potentially hazardous.

EXERCISE REGULARLY

The Bio-Nutrionics Program recommends that to make the Nutrition Program effective you should burn off at least 150 calories each day (or 1,050 calories per week) through the physical activity of your choice. If a daily schedule is inconvenient, you can get the same results by exercising four times a week to burn off 250 calories at each session, again roughly equal to 1,050 calories per week. You may even work up to a half-hour a day, five days a week and eventually feel so good you'll want to extend the program even more to perhaps 1,500 to 2,000 exercise calories per week burned. The hardest part is getting started.

CHART YOUR PROGRESS

The chart included below is your guide to selecting the physical activities you enjoy the most. It explains how long you need to participate in each activity to burn off a specific number of calories. Keep a record of your workouts to make sure you reach that goal of 150 calories a day. If you lose your motivation just think how great you'll feel when you've finished. Remember, the nutrition and activity program work together to bring your high cholesterol down. Furthermore, if one of your goals is to combine weight loss with cholesterol reduction, exercise is essential to maintain body tone. Go to it!

Activity Recommendations

Activity	Approximate calories burned per hour
Backpacking, Hiking	450–500
Baseball, Softball	250–350
Basketball	350–400
Bicycling (5.5 mph)	200–350
Bicycling (13 mph)	600–650
Bowling	250–300
Calisthenics	250–300
Chopping Wood	250–300
Dancing, Fast	350–400
Dancing, Slow	250–300
Football	300–400
Gardening (light)	250–300
Golfing	250–300
Horseback Riding	250–400
Housework	250–300
Jogging (10 min./mi.)	550–650
Judo, Karate	250–300
Manual Labor	450–500
Rope Jumping	750–850
Rowing Machine	550–650
Running (7.5 min./mi.)	750–850
Shoveling	350–400
Skating	300–450
Skiing (Cross-country)	1,200

Activity Recommendations

Activity	Approximate calories burned per hour
Skiing (Downhill, 10 mph)	550–600
Soccer (Rugby)	350–450
Squash, Racquetball, Handball	400–600
Stair Climbing	900–1,000
Swimming (50 meters/min.)	750–850
Tennis (Doubles)	300–350
Tennis (Singles)	400–450
Volleyball	250–300
Weight Lifting	300–400
Walking (3 mph)	250–300
Walking (4.5 mph)	350–400
Yard Work (heavy)	350–400

Whatever You Do, Have Fun

There may be activities on the list that you have never tried and always wanted to. This is the time to give them a whirl. You have embarked on a life-style program to improve your health and your entire outlook on life. It will not only be good for you but it also will be fun!

7. The Bottom Line

YOU CAN PREVENT CHOLESTEROL OVERLOAD

Now it's your turn. Think of this as the first day of the rest of your life. Begin the preventive program that Bio-Nutrionics offers now and gain the benefits no matter what your age. Remember, no one knows when their cholesterol buildup begins or how rapidly it will progress. You can't feel it or see it. Doesn't it make better sense to alter your life-style now rather than trying to halt or reverse half a lifetime of artery damage after CHD has reached an advanced state?

Dr. David Blankenhorn of the Southern California School of Medicine has some good news. He claims that cholesterol buildup in arteries increases at the rate of 2 percent a year, but that it can be halted, and in some cases reversed. Blankenhorn says a reduction in the rate of increase to 1 percent a year will greatly reduce CHD risk. Dr. William E. Conner of the University of Oregon Medical School concurs with Dr. Blankenhorn. Conner coined the phrase "cholesterol overload" in a scientific paper published in *Preventive Medicine* almost fifteen years ago. He believes that both prevention and regression of coronary atherosclerosis can be expected through safe, effective, nutritional measures incorporated into an active life-style. And that is what *Bio-Nutrionics* is all about.

THE PROOF OF THE PROMISE

At the beginning of this book we promised you that our program would lower your high blood cholesterol without the aid of medication and make you feel stronger and more energetic than you have felt in years. Here's the proof of that guarantee. Researchers at Bio-Nutrionics in New York have just completed a comprehensive analysis of 168 people who have finished their first thirty days in the program. They range in age from fifteen to seventy-five with a mean age of forty-two. There were 104 males and 64 females. The results of their cholesterol reduction will be reported first, but there are impressive results in each of five additional areas and we'll tell you about those also.

Cholesterol

The average serum cholesterol for the entire group was reduced from 216 to 196, while some cholesterols were lowered as much as 33 percent. The average cholesterol reduction for the entire group was 10 percent. As mentioned previously, this translates into a decrease in CHD risk of 20 percent achieved in just thirty days. (For every 1 percent decrease in cholesterol, there is a 2 percent decline in cardiovascular risk.)

Also quite remarkable were some of the changes in blood cholesterol of certain individuals, for example:

A twenty-eight-year-old male entered the program with a cholesterol of 191; one month later it was at 160—a drop of 31 points.

A forty-five-year-old female began with a high cholesterol level of 246; thirty days later, after a 97-point drop, her reading was 167.

A fifty-seven-year-old male with an initial level of 227 dropped 42 points to 185 in four weeks.

Please look at the chart below and we will summarize these statistics in another way.

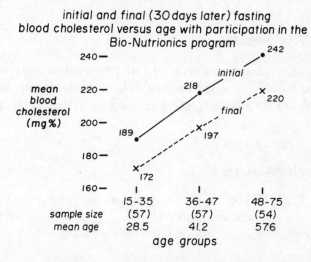

initial and final (30 days later) fasting
blood cholesterol versus age with participation in the
Bio-Nutrionics program

The solid line running diagonally across the chart shows the starting cholesterol levels of each of three age groups. The dotted line shows the readings for the same age groups after they completed the first thirty days. Please note that the group with 57.6-years mean age began with cholesterol levels averaging 242. Thirty days later their average was 220—just slightly higher than the 41.2-year-olds. It might be reasonable to conclude that a person could be about fifty-seven years of age going on forty-one after thirty days of the program— quite an arterial "rejuvenation"! And the forty-one-year-old can be made twenty-nine; that's a twelve-year "youthening"!

Just as we all accept that high cholesterol is a health hazard, there is increasing awareness that extremely low cholesterol levels may also be unhealthy. So it is gratifying to report that some low cholesterols were raised. For example, one thirty-eight-year-old male began the program with 103 and had an increase to 155—a 52-point increase; another male of fifty-one began at 109 and gained 51 points to reach 160.

Triglycerides

The beneficial effects of our program extend well beyond cholesterol reduction. The sample group had significant serum triglyceride reductions in the first thirty days.

Blood Glucose

The 168 participants enjoyed an average reduction of 5 percent in blood glucose levels. This reduction would be helpful in avoiding or controlling diabetes.

Blood Pressure

There was a statistically significant decrease in blood pressure with the average fifty-eight-year-old participant reverting to about thirty years of age as measured by systolic blood pressure.

Weight

The average body weight decreased from 167 pounds to 162 pounds in one month—better than a pound a week. This is quite a remarkable way to diet.

A Balancing of Many Factors

This is a critical concept and the evidence shows most clearly that the low cholesterol scores tended to rise, while the high scores seemed to decline. The result was that in one month there were fewer excessively low cholesterols. There were also fewer low and fewer high triglyceride values; blood glucose levels; systolic and diastolic blood pressure levels; and weight levels. This is the heart of the program; an individual biological makeup ultimately will reach a healthy mean.

MORE PROOF OF THE PROMISE

Here are the comments from a number of people who have continued on it.

Travel Agent: Female

"I began Bio-Nutrionics about nine months ago to lose weight and develop better eating habits. What resulted was more than I had hoped for. The program not only increased my awareness about nutrition, but it also made me feel good about myself. I particularly was pleased by the fact that I never had to feel like an outsider in business or social situations: I could have my glass of wine or a drink and not feel guilty. Best of all, I lowered my high blood cholesterol by sixty percent!"

Business Executive: Male

"I'm forty-five years old and unwilling to succumb to the deterioration associated with old age. I began Bio-Nutrionics simply to make me feel my very best. The results are amazing. The program has increased my energy, toned up my body, relieved a long-standing problem of sleeplessness, corrected improper elimination, and contributed unquestionably to a reduction in stress and an increase in psychological well-being. I weighed in at 186, and now three months later, my weight has stabilized at 170. Unlike conventional diets there has never been any sense of deprivation or hunger. The weight reduction seems related to balanced body chemistry and solid nutritional sense."

Office Employee: Female

"I had a weight problem and so far I have lost forty-six pounds in a little over four months. I've started to exercise, which I never did before in my life, and I have energy that is completely new to me. My cholesterol, which was high, is down . . . everything is down. I even went on a cruise in November and came home having lost two pounds."

Business Executive: Male

"Before beginning Bio-Nutrionics I thought I was doing a fair job keeping myself fit with respect to vitamins, nutrition, and exercise. But the program has heightened my awareness of these areas and really pulled them all together for me. For example, breakfast was never a part of my daily regimen and now it is. As a result, my alertness and attention to details during mornings at work has improved significantly. I'm six feet one and used to weigh between 195 and 200 pounds. Now my weight fluctuates between 185 and 190—quite a change. Bio-Nutrionics is an easy to follow, effective program that remains with you."

General Manager of a Famous New York City Hotel: Male

"I have a desire to stick with the program because I want to live a long life and enjoy the rewards of my hard work. My cholesterol was 215 when I started and five weeks later it was drastically reduced to 150. I play tennis regularly and within weeks I had more pep and energy and felt more alert both on the court and at work.

"Bio-Nutrionics takes self-commitment and self-discipline, like everything else in life, but it's worth it. To my amazement, I've reduced my weight from 162 to 152, which is perfect for my height and build, and my body fat, glucose, and total triglycerides have all gone down. I'm totally satisfied."

IT'S YOUR TURN TO PROVE THE PROMISE

Remember that for every 1 percent reduction in cholesterol, you decrease your risk for CHD by 2 percent. After just a few months on the program a 25 percent cholesterol reduction is a reality for many people. That means you will have cut your risk of coronary heart disease in half. We also guarantee you'll reach your maximum health potential—no matter who you are or what you do.

We hope you'll put our program to work right now—not for just a month but for a lifetime. Just give us a try and discover the difference between you . . . and you at your best.

Glossary

Artery: A tubular, branching, muscular, and elastic-walled vessel that carries blood away from the heart through the body.

Atherosclerosis: A degenerative disease characterized by abnormal thickening and hardening of the interior artery walls. As a result, the artery is reduced in size, impairing blood flow needed for every cell and increasing the risk for coronary heart disease (CHD).

Carbohydrate: A compound found in plants and animals and made up of carbon, hydrogen, and oxygen. In the body carbohydrates are broken down to simple sugars which provide energy. One gram of carbohydrate provides four calories.

Cholesterol: A fatty alcohol synthesized by the liver and obtained from animal products in our diets. Cholesterol is found in all cells and is necessary for life.

Coronary Heart Disease (CHD): A term often used interchangeably with coronary artery disease and cardiovascular disease. All three terms refer to diseases of the heart and artery system.

Fat: A complex compound composed of carbon, hydrogen, and oxygen. They are the most concentrated source of food energy, supplying nine calories per gram.

Fatty acids: The basic chemical unit in fats. There are three types with various characteristics.

Saturated fats: Fats of animal origin plus coconut and palm oil. They are generally solid at room temperature and chemically unreactive (contains no double bonds). A high intake of saturated fat has been linked to an increased risk of coronary heart disease.

Polyunsaturated and monounsaturated fats: Fats of vegetable origin that are liquid at room temperature and chemically reactive. Polyunsaturated fats contain more than one double bond, and monounsaturated fats contain one double bond. Both may help to decrease the risk of coronary heart disease and increased serum cholesterol.

Hydrogenated and partially hydrogenated fats: Unsaturated vegetable fats to which hydrogen has been added artificially to "saturate" the double bonds, rendering the fat nonreactive. They may be liquid or solid and act as a saturated fat in the body.

Fiber: Those components of foods that cannot be digested in the gastrointestinal tract of man. Fiber comes from plant sources and has many beneficial effects such as increasing stool bulk and decreasing cholesterol levels.

Hypertension: A disease characterized by blood pressure readings that are consistently above the normal range (high blood pressure).

Lipids: The technical name for fats.

Lipoproteins: Proteins combined with lipid components (cholesterol, phospholipid, triglycerides). There are various types.

High-density (HDL): These contain more protein than VLDL or LDL and carry cholesterol to the liver for excretion. A high HDL level has been shown to decrease the risk for CHD.

Low-density (LDL): Contain less protein than HDL. May increase the risk for CHD.

Very low-density (VLDL): Contain more lipid than protein and are the least dense of all lipoproteins. May increase the risk for CHD.

Omega-3 oils: A special group of polyunsaturated oils which have been shown to decrease the risk for CHD. Fish oils and linseed oil are two sources.

Omega-6 oils: A second group of polyunsaturated oils which also reduces the risk of CHD. Some common sources are sunflower, safflower, and corn oils.

Protein: A complex compound occurring in plants and animals and made up of carbon, hydrogen, oxygen, nitrogen, and other substances which are broken down in the body to amino acids. These amino acids are necessary for growth and repair of tissues and the regulation of bodily functions. One gram of protein will provide four calories.

Triglycerides: The visible fat in foods, the chief dietary and the major type of body fat. Triglycerides are synthesized by the liver from dietary fats (fatty acids) and glucose. High serum triglyceride levels are associated with increased risk of CHD.

A Personal Nutritionist for a Fraction of Normal Cost

With the supervision of a physician and the aid of our computer, we will design a personalized eating plan—a program of exercise and nutritional supplements that are tailored for you and no one else.

The program *costs a fraction of what celebrities, top athletes and others must pay for the same in-depth guidance.*

The program is as described in this book and much more. Your personal nutritionist has a series of meetings with you and consults with you by phone. Much of your past medical record, your likes and dislikes in food and physical activity, and your life-style goes into our computer. A 40- to 50-page printout of analysis and recommendation from your personal nutritionist, supervised by a physician, goes to you. It's instantly available to any doctor, specialist, hospital, or clinic you wish. You can update regularly. Vitamin and mineral supplements are blended to your unique needs. A sample is free. There's much more. Contact us.

DOCTORS—Write Stanley J. Leifer, president, for details of the BIO-NUTRIONICS plan to work jointly with doctors, nutritionists, hospitals, clinics in your location.

BIO-NUTRIONICS started in New York City. It now has opened offices in nearby areas and is expanding nationally, perhaps to your area.

For information on any of the above and the latest Bio-Nutrionics newsletter *free*, phone 1-800-STAMINA or write Dept. 62B, BIO-NUTRIONICS, 120 East 56th Street, New York, NY 10022.

About the Authors

Dr. Emanuel Cheraskin and Dr. Neil S. Orenstein are staff consultants to Bio-Nutrionics, Inc.

Dr. Cheraskin is the author of the bestselling *Psychodietics, the Vitamin C Connection* and hundreds of professional publications. He is a very active consultant to research organizations throughout the country and is professor emeritus at the University of Alabama at Birmingham.

Dr. Orenstein, a noted nutritional biochemist, has been on the staffs of Massachusetts General Hospital, Harvard Medical School, and Beth Israel Hospital in Boston. He is currently president of Commonwealth Nutrition, Inc., a nonprofit organization dedicated to nutrition, education, and research. He is also a consultant in nutritional biochemistry.

Paul L. Miner is a writer/producer/broadcaster of health, diet, and exercise features. These radio features, known as "Mr. Information," are broadcast ten times a week. He also owns and operates the Lincoln Company, an advertising and marketing firm located in Baltimore, MD.

Bio-Nutrionics, Inc., is a public company traded on NASDAQ—symbol BNUI.

Bibliography

Anderson, J. T., F. Grande, and A. Keys. Cholesterol-lowering diets. *J. Am. Diet Assoc.* 62 (1973): 133–142.

Anderson, J. W., W.J.L. Chen, and B. Sieling. Hypolipidemic effects of high-carbohydrate, high-fiber diets. *Metabolism* 29 (1980): 551–558.

Arky, R. A. "Hyperlipoproteinemia" in *Medicine (Metabolism)* Ed. by E. Rubenstein and D. Federman. Scientific American, Inc., 1984.

Barry, H. O., et al. The composition of the Eskimo food in Northwestern Greenland. *American Journal Clin. Nutrition* 33 (1980): 2657–2661.

Blankenhorn, D. N. The rate of atherosclerosis change during treatment of hyperlipoprothemia. *Circulation* (1978): 57(2): 355–361.

Brown, M. S., and J. L. Goldstein. Lipoprotein receptors in the liver: Cartel signals for plasma dilestene traffic. *Journal Clin. Invest.* (1983): 72:743–747.

Burr, M. L., and P. M. Sweetnam. Vegetarianism, dietary fiber and mortality. *Am. J. Clin. Nutri.* 36 (1982): 873–877.

Burt, A. O., and M. M. Burr. A new deficiency disease produced by the rigid exclusion of fat from the diet. *O. Biol. Chem.* (LXXXII) (2) (1929): 345–367.

Castelli, W. P., R. D. Abbott, and P. M. McNamara. Summary estimates of cholesterol used to predict coronary heart disease. *Circulation* 67 (1983): 730–734.

Consensus Conference. Lowering blood cholesterol to prevent heart disease. *JAMA* 253 (1985): 2080–2086.

Deliconstantinos, G. Free cholesterol not carried by lipoproteins in human serum. *Esperentia* 39 (1983): 748–750.

Ebert, R. V., and M. E. McNabb. Cessation of smoking in prevention and treatment of cardiac and pulmonary disease. *Arch. Intern. Med.* 144 (1984): 1558–1559.

Froelicher V., A. Battler, and M. D. McKirnan. Physical activity and coronary heart disease. *Cardiol.* 65 (1980): 153–190.

Garrison, R. J., P. W. Wilson, W. P. Castelli, M. Feinleib, W. B. Kennel, and P. M. McNamara. Obesity and lipoprotein cholesterol in the Framingham offspring study. *Metab.* 29 (1980): 1053–1060.

Gillum, R. F., A. R. Folson, and H. Blackburn. Decline in coronary heart disease mortality; old questions and new facts. *Amer. J. Med.* 76 (1984): 1055–1065.

Goldman, L., and E. F. Cook. The decline in ischemic heart disease mortality rates. *Ann. Inter. Med.* 101 (1984): 825–836.

Goldstein, J. L., et al. Hyperlipidemiac in coronary heart disease. I. Lipid levels in 500 survivors of myocardial infarction. *Journal Clin. Invest.* 52 (1973): 1544–1568.

Goldstein, J. L., and M. S. Brown. Familial hypercholesterolemia: pathogenesis of a receptor disease. *The*

Johns Hopkins Medical Journal 143 (1978): 8–16.

Gordan, T., W. P. Castelli, and M. C. Hjotland, et al. High density lipoprotein as a protective factor against coronary heart disease: The Framingham Study. *American Journal of Medicine* 62 (1977): 707.

Gresham, G. A. Is atheroma a reversible lesion? *Atheroscler.* 23 (1976): 379–391.

Grundy, S. M. Absorption and metabolism of dietary cholesterol. *American Rev. Nutr.* 3 (1983): 71–96.

Grundy, S. M. Hyperlipoproteinemia: Metabolic basis and rationale for therapy. *American Journal Cardiology* 54 (1984): 20C–28C.

Haskell, W. L., C. Camargo, P. T. Williams, Vranizank, R. Krauss, F. T. Lindgren, and P. D. Wood. The effect of cessation and resumption of moderate alcohol intake on serum high-density lipoprotein subfractions. *N. Eng. J. Med.* 310 (1984): 805–810.

Heyden S., and R. S. Williams. Cholesterol controversy—where do we go from here. *1 Cardiology* 69 (1982): 110–122.

Hopkins, P. N., and R. R. Williams. A survey of 246 suggested coronary risk factors. *Atherosclerosis* 40 (1981):1–52.

Hill-Berg, L. Lipid measurements for coronary risk assessment: a review. *Am. J. Tech.* 47 (1981): 539–543.

Hostmark, A. T. Physical activity and plasma lipids. *Scand. J. Soc. Med.* 29 (1982): 83–91.

Kay, R. M., Z. I. Sabry, and A. Csima. Multivariate analysis of diet and serum lipids in normal men. *Am. J. Clin. Nutr.* 33 (1980): 2566–2572.

Kesaniemi, Y. A., and S. M. Grundy. Increases low-density lipoprotein production associated with obesity. *Arteriosclerosis* 3 (1983): 170–177.

Kesaniemi, Y. A., and S. M. Grundy. Overproduction of low-density lipoprotein associated with CHD. *Arteriosclerosis* 3 (1983): 40–46.

Kninman, J. T., and C. E. West. The concentration of cholesterol in serum and in various serum lipoproteins in macrobiotic, vegetarian and nonvegetarian men and boys. *Atheroscler.* 43 (1982): 71–82.

Kofte, T. E. Risk factor control in coronary heart disease. Who needs it? *Postgrad. Med.* (1985): 233–245.

Krehl, W. A. The nutritional epidemiology of cardiovascular disease. *Anna. NY Acad. Sci.* 30 (1977): 335–359.

Kummeron, F. A. Dietary recommendations to reduce cholesterol consumption may have undesirable consequences. *Arterial wall,* VII (1981): 3–5.

Lewis, B. Dietary recommendations for coronary heart disease prevention: implications for non-cardiovascular disease. *Z. Ernahrungswiss* 22 (1983): 147–156.

Lipid Research Clinics Program. The lipid research clinics coronary primary prevention trial results I. Reduction in incidence of coronary heart disease. *JAMA* 251 (1984): 351–364.

Lipid Research Clinics Program. The lipid research clinics coronary primary trial results II. The relationship of reduction in incidence of coronary heart disease to cholesterol lowering. *JAMA* 251 (1984): 365–374.

Malmros, H. Lifestyle and risk factor trends, mortality trends, and public health perspectives. *Preventive Med.* 12 (1983): 204–209.

Martin, D. W., P. A. Mayes, and V. W. Roxell. *Harper's Review of Biochem-*

istry. Los Altos, CA: Lange Medical Publications, 1984.

Menotti, A., S. Conti, F. Dima, S. Giampaoli, B. Giuli, M. Matano, and F. Seccareccia. Incidence of coronary heart disease in two generations of men exposed to different levels of risk factors. *Acta Cardiologica* 60 (1985): 307–314.

Miller, W. W. Preventive cardiology for coronary artery disease. *Primary Care* 12 (1985): 15–38.

Morris, J. N., R. Pollard, M. G. Everitt, and S. P. W. Chave. Vigorous exercise in leisure-time: protection against coronary heart disease. *Lancet* (1980): 1207–1210.

Neufeld, H. N., and V. Goldboart. Coronary heart disease; genetic aspects. *Circulation* 67 (1983): 943–954.

Norum, K. R., T. Berg, P. Helgerud, and C. A. Drevon. Transport of cholesterol. *Physiol. Rev.* 63(4) (1983): 1343–1419.

Oldridge, N. B. Compliance and exercise in primary and secondary prevention of coronary heart disease: a review. *Prev. Med.* 11 (1982): 56–70.

Oliver, M. F. Should we not forget about mass control of coronary risk factors? *Lancet* (1983): 37–38.

Oliver, M. F. Lack of impact of prevention on sudden cardiac death. *J. Am. Coll. Cardiol.* 5 (1985): 150B–154B.

Oliver, M. F. Strategy, yield and risks of controlling plasma lipids in the primary prevention of coronary heart disease. *Adv. Exp. Med. Biol.* 183 (1985): 225–240.

Peng, S. K., and C. B. Taylor. Cholesterol autoxidation, health and atherosclerosis. *Wld. Rev. Ntr. Diet* 44 (1984): 117–154.

Pirie, P., R. Luepker, D. Jacobs, J. W. Brown, and N. Hall. Development and validation of a self-scoring test for coronary heart disease risk. *J. Commun. Health* 9 (1983): 65–71.

Pyorala, K., F. H. Epstein, and M. Kormtzer. Changing trends in coronary heart disease mortality; possible explanations. *Cardiology* 72 (1985): 5–10.

Quintao, E., S. M. Grundy, and E. H. Ahrens, Jr. Effects of dietary cholesterol on the regulation of food body digested in man. *J. Lipid Res.* 12(2) (1971): 233–247.

Rainville, S., and P. Vaccaro. Lipoprotein cholesterol levels, coronary artery disease and regular exercise: a review. *Mer. Corr. Ther. J.* 37 (1983): 161–165.

Rogotti, N. A., G. S. Thomas, and A. Leaf. Exercise and coronary heart disease. *Ann. Rev. Med.* 34 (1983): 391–412.

Roberts, W. C. Reducing the blood cholesterol level reduces the risk of heart attack. *Am. J. Cardiol.* 53 (1984): 649.

Robertson, F. The genetic component in coronary heart disease—a review. *Genet. Res. Camb.* 37 (1981): 1–16.

Rosenman, R. H., and M. A. Chesney. The relationship of Type A behavior pattern to coronary heart disease. *Activ. Nerv. Sup.* 22 (1980): 1–45.

Royce, S. M., R. P. Holmes, T. Takagi, and F. Kummerow. The influence of dietary isomeric and saturated fatty acids on atherosclerosis and eicosanoid synthesis in swine. *Am. J. Clin. Nutr.* 39 (1984): 215–222.

Schaefer, E. J., and R. I. Levy. Pathogenesis and management of lipoprotein disorders. *N. Eng. J. Med.* 312 (1985): 1300–1310.

Seeling, M. S. *Magnesium deficiency in the pathogenesis of disease; early roots of* cardiovascular, skeletal, and renal abnormalities. New York: Plenum Publishing Corporation, 1980.

Shekelle, R. B. Diet, serum cholesterol and death from coronary heart disease. New Eng. J. of Medicine 304(2) (1981): 65–70.

Simons, L. A. The lipid hypothesis is proven. Med. J. Austral. 140 (1984): 316–317.

Solberg, L. A., and J. P. Strong. Risk factors and atherosclerosis lesions— a review of autopsy studies. Atheroscler. 3 (1983): 187–198.

Stamler, J. Diet and coronary heart disease. Biometrics (1982): 95–114.

Stamler, J. The marked decline in coronary heart disease mortality rates in the United States, 1968–1981; summary of findings and possible explanations. Cardiology 72 (1985): 11–22.

Stryer, L. Biochemistry. San Francisco: W. H. Freeman and Co., 1975. Chapter 20.

Superko, H. R., P. D. Wood, and W. L. Haskell. Coronary heart disease and risk factor modification; is there a threshold? Am. J. Med. 78 (1985): 826–838.

Tashev, T. Nutrition and chronic disease. Nutrition in health and disease and international development: Symposium from the XII International Congress of Nutrition, 1981, Alan R. Liss, Inc., Publisher, 783–790.

Walker, W. J. Risk factor modification and coronary artery disease. JACC 2 (1983): 400.

Walker, S. P. Prevention for multifactoral diseases. Am. J. Epidemiol. 112 (1980): 409–416.

Watkins, L. O. Why are death rates from coronary heart disease decreasing? Postgraduate Med. 75 (1984): 201–214.

Wilhelmsen, L. Risk factors for coronary heart disease in perspective. Am. J. Med. (1984): 37–40.

Williams, P. T., P. D. Wood, W. L. Haskell, and K. Vranizan. The effects of running mileage and duration on plasma levels. JAMA 247 (1982): 2674–2679.

Williams, P. T., P. D. Wood, Vranizanki, J. J. Albers, S. C. Garay, and C. B. Taylor. Coffee intake and elevated cholesterol and apolipoprotein B levels in men. JAMA 253 (1985): 1407–1411.

Williams, P. T., W. L. Haskell, K. M. Vranizan, S. N. Blair, R. M. Krauss, H. R. Superko, J. J. Albers, B. Frey-Hewitt, and P. D. Wood. Associations of resting heart rate with concentrations of lipoprotein subfractions in sedentary men. Circulation 71 (1985): 441–449.

Wilson, P. W., R. D. Abbott, R. J. Garrison, and W. P. Castelli. Estimation of very low-density lipoprotein cholesterol from data on triglyceride concentration in plasma. Clin. Chem. 27 (1981): 2008–2010.

Wood, P. D., R. B. Terry, and W. L. Haskell. Metabolism of substrates: diet, lipoprotein metabolism, and exercise. Federation Proc. 44 (1985): 358–363.

Wood, P. D., P. T. Williams, and W. L. Haskell. Physical activity and high-density lipoproteins. In Clinical and Metabolic Aspects of High-density Lipoproteins edited by N. E. Miller and G. J. Miller, pp. 133–165.

Wyndham, C. H. The role of physical activity in the prevention of ischaemic heart disease: a review. SA Med. J. (1979): 7–13.